REAL-WORLD MATHEMATICS THROUGH SCIENCE

IN THE AIR

CHRISTINE V. JOHNSON

Nancy Cook, Project Director

Developed by Washington MESA

INNOVATIVE LEARNING PUBLICATIONS

ADDISON-WESLEY PUBLISHING COMPANY

Menlo Park, California • Reading, Massachusetts • New York
Don Mills, Ontario • Wokingham, England • Amsterdam • Bonn
Paris • Milan • Madrid • Sydney • Singapore • Tokyo
Seoul • Taipei • Mexico City • San Juan

MESA wishes to express its appreciation to the following people for their advice and assistance, without which this module could not have been completed:

Nancy Cook, Ph.D.
Washington MESA
University of Washington
Seattle, Washington

Christine V. Johnson
Washington MESA
University of Washington
Seattle, Washington

Susan Darcy
Boeing Test Pilot
Seattle, Washington

K. C. Chapin
Wings Aloft
Aircraft Flying School
Seattle, Washington

Washington MESA middle school mathematics and science teachers in Seattle, Spokane, Tacoma, Toppenish, and Yakima, Washington

Project Editor: Katarina Stenstedt
Production/Manufacturing: Leanne Collins
Design Manager: Jeff Kelly
Text Design: Michelle Taverniti
Text Illustration: Carl Yoshihara
Cover Design: Dennis Teutschel
Cover Photograph: © Stephen Wilkes, The Image Bank

Photographs: 53 Susan Darcy, 74 Darrell R. Wagner
The illustrations on pages 17, 39, and 45 are based on material from *The Complete Private Pilot*. Copyright ©1992 Aviation Supplies and Academics, Inc.

This book is published by Innovative Learning Publications™, an imprint of the Alternative Publishing Group of Addison-Wesley Publishing Company.

This material in part is based on work supported by Grant No. MDR–8751287 from the National Science Foundation; Instructional Materials Development; 1800 G Street NW; Washington, DC 20550. The material was designed and developed by Washington MESA (Mathematics, Engineering, Science Achievement); 353 Loew Hall FH-18; University of Washington; Seattle, WA 98195. Any opinions, findings, conclusions, or recommendations expressed in this publication are those of Washington MESA and do not necessarily reflect the views of the National Science Foundation.

ISBN 0–201–49311-X

3 4 5 6 7 8 9 10–DR–99 98 97 96 95

IN THE AIR

CONTENTS

INTRODUCTION

In the Air is one of the middle-grades instructional modules created and field-tested by the Washington MESA (Mathematics, Engineering, Science Achievement) project. Washington MESA operates on the premise that effective classroom materials should facilitate connections between classroom and real-world mathematics and science. Staff members and teachers work with scientists, mathematicians, and engineers to outline each module. Pilot modules are tested in middle school classrooms, then revised using feedback from the teachers.

The modules combine important mathematics themes with relevant, exciting science topics. The activities are based on current reform philosophies recommended by the National Council of Teachers of Mathematics' (NCTM's) *Curriculum and Evaluation Standards for School Mathematics* and the American Association for the Advancement of Science's *Project 2061.* Students will

◆ learn by doing. Applying newly-introduced mathematics skills, students plan a cross-country flight, using a state map as an aeronautical chart.

◆ employ a variety of reasoning processes by using several mathematical approaches to solve similar problems.

◆ learn to express technical concepts as they write and discuss answers to open-ended questions. The questions are designed to provoke further thought about how science and mathematics connect to the everyday world.

◆ learn the appropriate use of calculators by solving real problems. Students are taught how to conceptualize and set up problems that they can then solve using calculators.

◆ make connections between mathematics and science as well as within mathematics and science. Writing Link, History Link, Interest Link, and Technology Link activities are included to expand the connections to other subject areas.

◆ explore careers by simulating professional roles in the activities. Students also study jobs that use mathematics and science in the Career Link features.

In the Air directs middle school students toward active involvement in learning. Students emulate real-world work environments by collaborating in small groups and striving for group consensus. They work with concrete materials and evaluate open-ended problems—the combination that helps the transition from concrete to abstract thinking crucial to the intellectual development of students at this age. To ascertain that instruction is working, assessment is integrated into *In the Air* activities. Assessment and instruction are identical.

Family encouragement can help students to succeed educationally, so a special activity involves students' families in hands-on, collaborative work. Students learn as they work with parents and other family members to determine airspeed and plot navigational courses for paper airplanes.

Each activity begins with an Overview page summarizing what students will be doing and how the teacher needs to prepare. This is followed by background information for the teacher's use and a Presenting the Activity section, which describes the activity in detail and suggests discussion questions and assessment strategies. The activities also include Student Sheets and Transparency Masters in blackline master form (completed Student Sheets are provided on pages 81–88). Career Link, History Link, Writing Link, Technology Link, and Interest Link features are found throughout the book.

CONCEPTUAL OVERVIEW

In the Air addresses the following mathematics topics, science topics, and NCTM standards.

NCTM Curriculum Standards

Problem Solving
  Open-Ended
  Multiple Strategies
Communication
  Verbal and Written
Reasoning
  Logical and Spatial
  Predictions and Evaluations
Mathematical Connections
  Among Topics
  To Real-World Contexts

NCTM Teaching Standards

Worthwhile Tasks
  Real-World Contexts
Teacher's Role
  Listening and Observing
  Orchestrating Discourse
Enhancement Tools
  Calculators
  Concrete Materials
Learning Environment
  Collaborative Work

NCTM Evaluation Standards

Alignment
  Integral to Instruction
Multiple Sources
  Oral and Written
  Individual and Group
Multiple Methods
  Instructional Planning
  Grading
Mathematical Power
  Communicate
  Reason
  Integrate
  Generalize

Mathematics Content

Number Relationships
  Percents
Computation and Estimation
  Mental Arithmetic
  Calculators
  Estimation
Patterns and Functions
  Functional Relations
Algebra
  Equations
Geometry
  Angles
  Scale Drawings
Measurement
  Angle Measures
  Distances
  Conversions

Statistics
  Data Collection
  Tables
  Averages
  Graphs
  Inferences

Science Topics

Navigation
  Magnetic Compass
  Compass Rose
  Orientation
  Compass Headings
  Cardinal Directions
  Intercardinal
    Directions

Map Reading
  City Maps
  State Maps
  Map Scales
  Giving and Reading
    Directions
Paper Airplanes
  Designing Process
  Testing Process
Physics
  Speed, Distance, and
    Time
Scientific Process
  Predicting
  Hypothesizing
  Analyzing
  Concluding

ACTIVITY OVERVIEW

Overview

Many middle school students know how to use city and state maps for travel, and they may be familiar with linear and angle measurement, distance, and rates. However, they are probably unfamiliar with the mathematics of aeronautical navigation and the related careers of a pilot or aeronautical engineer.

In the Air gives students a sampling of activities and navigational techniques to explore while introducing them to career aspects of a visual flight pilot. It emphasizes the mathematical connections for charting a cross-country journey in a Cessna 172.

If possible, invite a pilot or aeronautical engineer to visit the class. Students could ask about other aspects of a career in aeronautics.

Activity 1: Navigation

Students begin to explore navigation by using a city map. They follow a prepared set of instructions to determine the unknown destination. After selecting a city park, they write out specific travel instructions for another group to navigate and solve. The magnetic compass is introduced, and students explore its use in determining direction in navigation. Students do an orientation activity to learn to use angle measurement to convey and determine direction.

Activity 2: Roses

The compass rose is introduced and students learn that navigation In the Air follows essentially the same process as navigating on the ground. They learn that degrees are a basic unit of navigation, and they explore the various patterns and mathematical relationships in the degree measures on a compass rose. They use a circular protractor to interpret as well as to draw angles representing compass headings for several courses.

Activity 3: Destination, Direction, and Distance

Students are introduced to the three basics of navigation: destination, direction, and distance. Students use a state map to investigate the process involved in charting and navigating an aeronautical course. They draw course-lines between starting points and destinations, determine directions, and calculate distances based on the mileage scale.

Activity 4: Distance, Speed, and Time

Students investigate the relationships among distance, speed, and time. They explore the mathematics of rate problems involving these variables as important aspects of preparing a flight plan. With their group, they develop a formula which gives the relationship, and then they apply it in making typical flight plan decisions.

Activity 5: Dead Reckoning

This activity represents a culmination and application of the mathematical concepts and navigational skills developed in the previous activities. Working in pairs, students use the process of dead reckoning to chart an aeronautical course on a state map. They prepare a detailed flight plan to satisfy criteria for a cross-country venture in a Cessna 172 that will involve at least three stops before returning home. Then they examine an aeronautical sectional chart in their groups, locate familiar landmarks, and interpret some of the various symbols used. They compare their charted cross-country courses on state maps to their courses as they would appear on an aeronautical sectional.

Family Activity: Paper Plane Predictions

With their families, students design paper airplanes. Students and their families apply the concepts of distance, speed, and time to the aerodynamics of paper airplanes. Based on the results of several test flights, each family determines its plane's average airspeed in feet per second. They use this information to expand, represent, and interpret their results graphically. They determine the time it will take their paper airplanes to fly from home to school.

MATERIALS LIST

The following is a consolidated list of materials needed for *In the Air*. A list of materials needed for each activity is included in the Overview for each activity.

Activity	Materials Required
Navigation	*For each student:* ◆ Student Sheets 1.1–1.3 ◆ Directions (prepared by the teacher) ◆ Ruler *For each group of students:* ◆ City map (see Background Information, page 3) ◆ At least one magnetic compass *For the teacher:* ◆ Aeronautical chart (see Background Information, page 3) ◆ Transparencies of Student Sheets 1.1–1.3 (optional) ◆ Transparency Master 1.4 ◆ Transparency Master 1.5 (optional) ◆ Transparency pen
Roses	*For each student:* ◆ Student Sheets 2.1–2.3 ◆ Circular protractor ◆ Straightedge *For each group of students:* ◆ City map *For the teacher:* ◆ Transparencies of Student Sheets 2.1–2.3 (optional) ◆ Transparency Master 2.4 ◆ Transparency pen

Activity	Materials Required
Destination, Direction, and Distance	*For each student:* ◆ Student Sheets 3.1–3.4 ◆ Directions (prepared by the teacher) *For each group of students:* ◆ Laminated state maps (1 per pair of students) ◆ Sponge or paper towel ◆ Circular protractor (1 per pair of students) ◆ Centimeter ruler (1 per pair of students) ◆ Transparency pen ◆ At least one calculator ◆ Spray bottle of water ◆ Meter stick *For the teacher:* ◆ Transparency of a state map ◆ Transparency pen ◆ Transparencies of Student Sheets 3.1–3.4 (optional) ◆ Aeronautical sectional chart (optional) ◆ Globe or Transparency Master 3.5
Distance, Speed, and Time	*For each student:* ◆ Student Sheets 4.1–4.3 *For each group of two students:* ◆ Laminated state map ◆ Sponge or paper towel ◆ Circular protractor ◆ Ruler ◆ Transparency pen ◆ Calculator ◆ Spray bottle of water ◆ Meter stick *For the teacher:* ◆ Transparencies of Student Sheets 4.1–4.3 and a transparency pen (optional)

Activity	Materials Required

Dead Reckoning

For each student:
◆ Student Sheet 5.1

For each group of two students:
◆ Laminated state map
◆ Sponge or paper towel
◆ Circular protractor
◆ Ruler
◆ Transparency pen
◆ Calculator
◆ Spray bottle of water
◆ Meter stick
◆ Aeronautical sectional chart

For the teacher:
◆ Transparency of Student Sheet 5.1 (optional)

Paper Plane Predictions

For each family:
◆ Family Activity Sheets 1–4
◆ 8.5" × 11" paper
◆ Scissors (optional)
◆ Tape (optional)
◆ Carpenter's tape measure
◆ Stopwatch
◆ Calculator
◆ Straightedge
◆ Student Sheet 2.3 (optional, for reference)

For the teacher:
◆ Transparency Master
◆ Transparency pen

RESOURCES LIST

This list of resources was compiled by teachers, scientists, and professionals who participated in developing *In the Air*. It is intended for teachers who would like to pursue the topic further with their class, with small groups of students who are particularly interested in the topic, with individual students who desire further investigations, or for professional development.

1. Aviator Store
   7201 Perimeter Rd. S., Boeing Field
   Seattle, WA 98108
   (206) 763-0666

2. Wings Aloft
   Aircraft Flying School
   8467 Perimeter Rd. S., Boeing Field
   Seattle, WA 98108
   (206) 763-2113

3. National Oceanic and Atmospheric Administration (NOAA)
   Distribution Division
   66501 Lafayette Avenue
   Riverdale, MD 20840
   (301) 436-6990

4. C-Thru Ruler Company
   6 Britton Drive
   Bloomfield, Connecticut 06002
   (203) 243-0303

5. King of the Road Map Service, Inc.
   P. O. Box 55758
   Seattle, WA 98155
   (800) 223-8852

6. Federal Aviation Administration, ANM-14A
   Northwest Aviation Education Officer
   1601 Lind Avenue SW
   Renton, WA 98055-4056
   (206) 227-2079

7. American Institute of Aeronautics and Astronautics
   Student Programs Department
   The Aerospace Center
   370 L'Enfant Promenade SW
   Washington, DC 20024-2518
   (202) 646-7458

8. Tuskegee Airmen, Inc.
   Tuskegee Airmen Museum, Historic Fort Wayne
   Detroit, MI 48283

9. "The 'White Pelican' Project." American Institute of Aeronautics and Astronautics's *AIAA Student Journal,* Summer (1992), pp. 6–10.

10. Gardner, Robert. *The Complete Private Pilot*. Renton, Wash.: Aviation Supplies and Academics, Inc., 1992.

11. *Flight Training Handbook*. Washington, D.C.: Federal Aviation Administration, 1980.

12. Maloney, Elbert S. *Dutton's Navigation and Piloting*. Annapolis, Md.: Naval Institute Press, 1978.

13. Dye, Aimee. *Aviation Curriculum Guide for Middle School Level*. Washington, D.C.: Federal Aviation Administration, 1984.

14. Mander, Jerry, George Dippel, and Howard Gossage. *The Great International Paper Airplane Book*. New York: Simon and Schuster, 1967.

ACTIVITY
1

NAVIGATION

Overview

Using a city map, students follow a prepared set of instructions to determine the unknown destination. After selecting a city park, they write out specific travel instructions for another group to navigate and solve. Students explore the magnetic compass and its use in determining direction in navigation. They do an orientation activity to learn about the use of angle measurement to convey and determine direction.

Purpose. Students begin to understand the processes used when navigating on land. They recognize the importance of angle measurement to convey and determine position and direction.

Time. One to two 40- to 50-minute periods.

Materials. *For each student:*

◆ Student Sheets 1.1–1.3

◆ Directions (prepared by the teacher)

◆ Ruler

For each group of students:

◆ City map (see Background Information, page 3)

◆ At least one magnetic compass

For the teacher:

◆ Aeronautical chart (see Background Information, page 3)

◆ Transparencies of Student Sheets 1.1–1.3 (optional)

◆ Transparency Master 1.5 (optional) and Transparency Master 1.4

◆ Transparency pen

Getting Ready

1. Locate city maps and an aeronautical chart. See Resources List (page xiv).

2. Locate magnetic compasses, rulers, and transparency pen.

3. Write a set of directions to travel from school to a familiar location in the city. See example in the Background Information.

4. Determine a location to conduct the compass walks.

5. Duplicate Student Sheets 1.1–1.3.

6. Prepare transparencies of Student Sheets 1.1–1.3 and Transparency Masters 1.5 (optional) and 1.4.

Background Information

Navigation is the theory and practice of determining both where you are and the course to get you where you want to go. Navigation is both an art and a science: an art because of the skills and techniques required and a science because it is based on the systematic application of physical laws. There are three basic problems involved in navigation, and this unit addresses each of them.

1) How do you determine position?

2) How do you determine the direction in which to proceed in order to get from one position to another?

3) How do you determine distance and the related factors of time and speed?

The study of navigation is learning how to measure and use position, direction, distance, time, and speed. The practice of navigation is the application of this knowledge.

For the most part, the techniques of navigation are universal and applicable to land, sea, or air travel. Navigation can be divided into four primary classifications: piloting, dead reckoning, celestial navigation, and radio navigation. These are not only convenient categories, but also the sequence in which they originated over the centuries.

Piloting, or pilotage, means determining position by using frequent or continuous reference to landmarks. For example, street names and familiar places on maps guide travelers on land. For air travel, pilotage involves planning the course on an aeronautical chart and then flying from one visible landmark to another.

The name *dead reckoning* comes from the term *deduced reckoning*. *Deduced* is abbreviated to "ded" and pronounced "dead." In the early days of sailing, mariners kept track of their position as accurately as possible by estimating their speed and the effects of wind and current and by having a deduced reckoning of where they had traveled since their last known position. When pilots plan their flights by dead reckoning, they determine a course-line, allow for wind direction and speed, derive a heading and a ground speed, and estimate a time of arrival at the destination. The most common form of navigation for small planes is a combination of dead reckoning and pilotage.

The first step in navigation is having the proper map or chart. A map is a representation on a flat surface of a portion of the earth's surface. It may show physical features (cities, towns, and roads), political boundaries, and other geographic information. An aeronautical chart is a specialized map that has been specifically designed for navigation. It is intended to be worked upon, not merely looked at, and should readily permit a graphic solution of a navigational problem such as determining distance or direction. Aeronautical charts emphasize landmarks and other features of special importance to pilots. Because of this, they appear cluttered and complicated. Students may initially be overwhelmed by the appearance of an aeronautical chart. For this reason, initially display at least one aeronautical chart prominently in the classroom, but wait until Activity 3, after students have had some experience with charting a course-line and determining direction on state maps, before you introduce aeronautical charts for groups to examine.

Aeronautical charts, known as sectionals, are updated and revised every six months. All obsolete charts are instantly recycled. Teachers can order canceled sectionals from the Distribution Division of NOAA (see Resources List, p. xiv). A letter stating that the chart is for classroom use and $2.00 per chart should accompany each request. Inquiries should be made several months in advance to assure delivery.

Throughout this unit, students will use city and state maps as alternatives to sectional charts. King of the Road Maps (see Resources List, p. xiv) will either give you these city maps, especially if you call them two to four months in advance, or charge you a nominal fee. Try not to submit your request during the summer because that is their busiest time.

One of the main uses of a map or chart is to find the direction from one point to another. Giving directions for traveling within a city usually requires following a series of street names interspersed with 90° turns. In these first activities, students will refresh their map-reading skills while they make discoveries about direction.

For Student Sheet 1.1, you will need to prepare a set of directions to lead students from their school to a familiar location they discover by following the route on a city map. Insert blanks in several appropriate places throughout the directions to encourage map reading and group discussions. For example, a possible route from Mercer Middle School in Seattle to the Boeing Museum of Flight is suggested below.

> Turn left on Columbia Way South. At the next block, turn right onto South Snoqualamie Street. In one block turn left onto 15th Avenue South. In approximately 0.8 miles it bends right and becomes (*Swift Avenue South*). At the first opportunity, turn right onto Albro Place, which takes you across (*I-5*). As you come down the overpass, Albro

Place bends into Ellis Avenue South. At the first light, in three blocks, turn left on East Marginal Way South. In approximately two miles you will see the (*Museum of Flight*) on the left side of the road, right on the edge of (*Boeing Field*).

On Student Sheet 1.1, students will estimate the distance from school to a city park. Most United States maps are scaled in inches. A typical city map might state 1.5 inches is equivalent to a mile. Students will need to determine the scale for the map they are using.

For an unknown reason, the earth is surrounded by a magnetic field that, unlike the force of gravity, is continually changing at a very slow rate. The magnetic compass is controlled by the lines of force in the earth's magnetic field. These lines are not parallel to the meridians; they diverge from the meridians at different angles in different locations on the earth's surface. The amount of this difference, or variation, is indicated on all aeronautical charts. Transparency Master 1.5 illustrates these lines of force and the location of magnetic north, which is about 1,400 miles from true north. The line passing through Chicago and Key West has no variation because it is aligned with both magnetic north and true north. East or west of that line, the angle between true and magnetic north increases.

Since all maps are based on true north, pilots determine course directions from true north, and then adjust their compass headings according to the magnetic variation in that area. A pilot in Los Angeles adds −14° (or subtracts 14°) from the true course; whereas a pilot in Philadelphia will add 10°. The variation in Oregon and Washington is about −20°.

In Activities 1 and 2, students will become familiar with plotting course-lines, determining direction from true north, and using a magnetic compass. Adjusting the course headings for magnetic variation is not necessary or recommended in this unit. Simply being aware of the phenomenon is sufficient.

Student Sheets 1.2 and 1.3 serve as an initial introduction to orienting and operating a magnetic compass. Again, for the purpose of this activity, there is no need to distinguish between true and magnetic north.

The Writing Link "Design Your Own Map" can be used at any time during the activity to stimulate student interest. The Interest Link "The Compass" is referred to in Assessment Question 4.

Presenting the Activity

City Maps. Divide your class into small working groups. Begin with a class discussion to define navigation. List student responses and incorporate them into a complete definition. If necessary, suggest that it simply means knowing where you are and how to determine a course to where you want to go.

Have students locate their school on a city map in their groups. Ask them if there is a special symbol to indicate schools. If so, why, and what is it? Suggest they locate their neighborhood and see if they can recognize and follow their route to school on the map.

When giving directions, people often use names of specific streets. They may mention certain buildings or familiar places as landmarks along the way. They might say, "Turn right at the light," or "Go three blocks and then turn left."

Distribute Student Sheet 1.1 and a set of prepared directions for question 3. Suggest they work in small groups as they become more familiar with following and giving directions using the city map.

After students have completed Student Sheet 1.1, conduct a class discussion of their routes. As a class, evaluate their clarity and validity, discuss if there is more than one route possible, and if so, decide if one route is shorter or more efficient than the others.

The Magnetic Compass. Distribute the magnetic compasses and Student Sheet 1.2. The first exercise allows groups to experiment with the compass.

After the groups have answered question 1, use Transparency Master 1.4 to discuss the parts of a compass. Elicit from the students that the red end of the magnetic needle points north and the white end points south. Explain that the dial, or compass housing, is a circular protractor divided into 360 equal parts, or degrees. Have students note that the four cardinal directions are indicated on the compass.

Have students determine the scale suggested by each line marked on the housing dial. Usually, each space represents 2°. Point out, if necessary, that the base plate is used to indicate the line of travel as shown by the "direction of travel" arrow on the plate.

Use Transparency Master 1.5 if you choose to indicate the location of magnetic north with respect to true north, which you might do if the topic arises from the students. Briefly explain how the magnetic compass is controlled by the lines of force in the earth's magnetic field. Tell students that the difference between magnetic north and true north at any location is called the magnetic variation.

Have the students complete Student Sheet 1.2, which provides experiences using a compass. The first step in using a compass is to orient it. To orient a compass is to know your location in relation to north. Suggest that students work in groups as they do the activities. Remind them to keep items of steel or iron away from the compass needle to avoid influencing it.

Travel by land, sea, and air all involve the use of navigation. When you travel by land, you can usually find your way by noticing signs and landmarks, looking for them on a map, or asking someone for directions. Navigating in the city is usually restricted to zigzagging from one place to another, using right turns to avoid buildings. Navigating by sea or air, however, has fewer restrictions. You must stay clear of rocks in the sea and mountains when flying, but the restriction to 90° turns to avoid buildings is gone. The last question on Student Sheet 1.2 addresses these differences. Students are asked to determine the direction they would use if they were to fly to school.

Once each group has finished the activities and has become familiar with the compass, they may proceed to Student Sheet 1.3, which provides further experiences with orienteering.

Discussion Questions

1. Why do directions and headings relate to true North?

2. What are the similarities and differences in navigating on land, sea, and air?

3. Why is a compass deemed one of the ten essential items to take on a hike? What do you suppose the others are?

Assessment Strategies

1. Work in groups of four. Have two members of your group stand in different places within the classroom and face the door. Are they heading in the same direction? Explain. Ask them each to slowly turn clockwise and face in the exact opposite direction. How far has each person turned? Is each one now facing the same destination? Why or why not? What does this have to do with navigating an airplane?

   Draw a picture which represents the above situation.

2. Write directions for a classmate to navigate from one location in the classroom to another.

3. Using another student's directions from (2), determine the desired destination. Critique the directions.

4. Read the Interest Link "The Compass." What are the advantages of a gyrocompass over a magnetic compass? What are some disadvantages? (Think about how the gyrocompass works.)

The Compass

In 700 B.C., the Greeks knew about a strange stone that could "pull" on iron. The stone, called *lodestone*, was magnetic. But it wasn't until about 2,000 years later that they learned how this stone could be used to help them navigate the open seas. Until then, sailors had to stay close to the land or watch the stars carefully (if it wasn't cloudy!) to find out where they were.

It's unknown where the compass was first used. The Chinese may have been using compasses long before the Europeans put them on their boats. It is thought that in the 1100s, someone put a sliver of lodestone in a bowl of water and discovered that the sliver always pointed north-south! How did the sliver of stone do this? The earth is like a magnet itself—with a north pole and a south pole. These magnetic poles are slightly different from the exact top and bottom of the earth, which are called the *true North Pole* and *true South Pole*. The earth creates a magnetic field. A magnetized needle that is free to turn (like a sliver of lodestone in water) always lines up with the earth's magnetic field.

The first compasses were made with needles of magnetized iron. The iron was magnetized by rubbing it against lodestone, then it was placed on a piece of wood or cork that floated in a bowl of water. Later, someone put the iron on a pivot and put markings on a card under the needle to divide the compass into 32 points of direction. When ships started being built out of metal in the 1800s, the metal interfered with the compass readings. What did the sailors do? Find out what you can about the gyrocompass to answer this question.

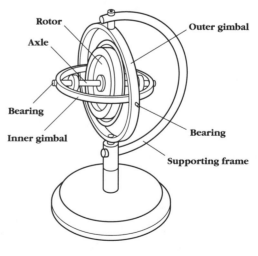

Design Your Own Map

Imagine that the people living in an area not far from your city want to make a "sister" city that is very much like yours. There are not enough people living there to make a city yet, but planners are sure it will grow just as your city did many years ago.

They want you to design a map of their city so when more people do move to the area (and start building structures and roads) everyone will know where things should go.

Using your city map as a reference, make a map for this city. Make sure you include all the important buildings, roads, scales, symbols, and so on that appear on your city map.

The new city will be about the same size as your city, but you can experiment and improve the way the city is laid out. Would the airport work better in a different part of town? How could you make the streets and roads easy to follow? Give names to the new city and its main streets. In a short essay, tell how navigation in this new city will be better than in yours.

City Maps

1. Locate your school on a city map.

2. Is your school located in the north, south, east, or west part of the city? Explain.

3. Using the city map, follow the written directions given to you. They begin at school and end at a familiar location.

   a. Describe the final destination.

   b. How did you know the destination?

4. When you make a right turn, how many degrees are you turning? Explain.

5. Choose a city park on the map. Its name is _____.

   a. Is it north, south, east, or west of the school? Explain.

   b. Write clear directions to travel by car from school to _____ park.

   c. Is there more than one route to this park? Why or why not?

   d. Determine the distance this park is from school. Explain.

City Maps

6. Have one person in your group join another group to read them the directions you wrote in question 5b.

7. Use the city map with the remaining group members to follow the step-by-step directions as they are read to you by another group's representative. Remember, their directions begin at school and end at a city park.

   a. According to your map, what park are they giving you directions to?

   b. Did you arrive at the intended destination? Why, or why not?

8. Locate your house on the map.

   a. Do you live in the north, south, east, or west part of town?

   b. Where is your house in relation to school?

   c. Determine the route you use to get home from school. Write it down.

   d. Give verbal directions on how you get home from school to the other members of your group while they look at the map.

   e. Did they arrive at your house? Why or why not?

9. Repeat (8) for another member of your group.

The Magnetic Compass

1. With your group, experiment with and examine the magnetic compass. Describe your findings.

2. Follow these steps to orient yourself toward magnetic north.
   a. Turn the compass dial until the travel arrow is lined up with 0° (north).
   b. Stand up and hold the compass in your hand near the center of your body with the direction of the travel arrow pointing straight ahead. Keep the compass level so the magnetic needle can swing freely.
   c. While holding the compass, turn yourself around with the compass until the red north end of the magnetic needle points to the letter N on the dial.
   d. Look up in the direction of the travel arrow. You are facing north. Describe something in your room that identifies the direction north.

   e. Do you agree with other groups? Why or why not?

3. Follow these steps to orient yourself toward a heading of 60°.
   a. Turn the dial and line up 60° with the direction of the travel arrow.
   b. Stand and hold the compass as before with the direction of the travel arrow pointing straight ahead.
   c. Turn around until the red north end of the magnetic needle points to the letter N on the dial.
   d. Look up in the direction of the travel arrow. You are now facing a 60° compass heading. Give a descriptor (describe what you are facing) in your room that identifies the direction of 60°.

   e. A compass heading is read clockwise from north. Explain what this means.

The Magnetic Compass

4. Adjust the magnetic compass and orient yourself to face

   a. due west. What is the compass heading? Give a descriptor of its direction.

   b. a 120° compass heading, and give a descriptor of its direction.

   c. a 340° compass heading, and give a descriptor of its direction.

   d. a compass heading of _____° (fill in the blank with a degree), and give a descriptor of its direction.

   e. Check your descriptors with those of another group. Do they agree? Explain.

5. Face a compass heading of 40°. Turn clockwise until you face the opposite direction.

   a. How do you know by looking at the compass that you have turned completely around?

   b. What direction do you think you are facing?

   c. What is the compass heading? Describe how you can adjust the compass to give you the correct compass heading.

6. Refer to your city map. Approximately what compass heading will a plane face to fly from school to the city park you selected on Student Sheet 1.1? Explain your reasoning.

Compass Walk

1. With your group, use a compass to go on a walk around the path described below.

   a. Place a marker on the ground to represent your starting point.

   b. Orient yourself in the direction of a 50° compass heading. Walk ten paces and stop. Place another marker at this location.

   c. Orient yourself in the direction of a 160° compass heading. Walk ten paces and stop. Place another marker at this location.

   d. In what direction do you need to orient yourself in order to return to your starting point?

   e. How many paces do you need to walk in order to arrive at your starting point?

   f. Sketch a picture of your walk, including the angles of orientation (the compass heading) at each step.

2. With your group, use a compass to walk the following path.

   a. Place a marker on the ground to represent your starting point.

   b. Orient yourself in the direction of a 40° compass heading. Walk ten paces and stop. Place a marker to designate your location.

   c. Orient yourself in the direction of a 220° compass heading. In what direction are you facing?

Compass Walk

d. Walk ten paces and stop. Where are you? Explain.

e. Sketch a picture of your walk.

3. What does this activity have to do with flying an airplane?

Magnetic Compass

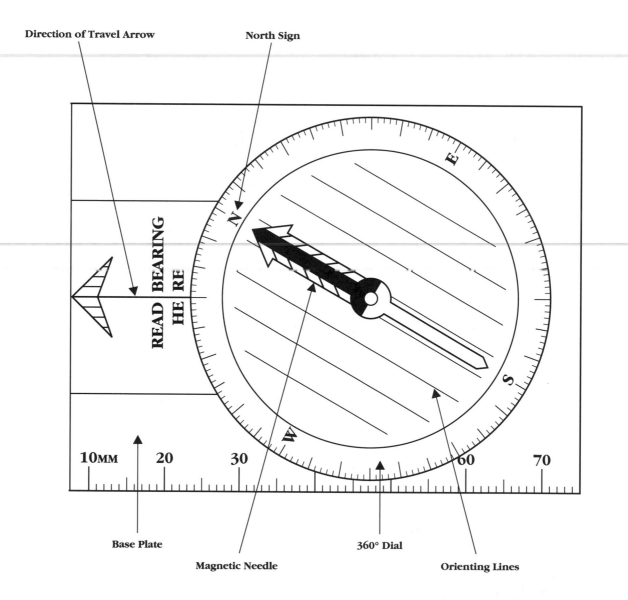

Direction of Travel Arrow

North Sign

READ BEARING HE RE

10MM 20 30 60 70

Base Plate

Magnetic Needle

360° Dial

Orienting Lines

Magnetic Fields

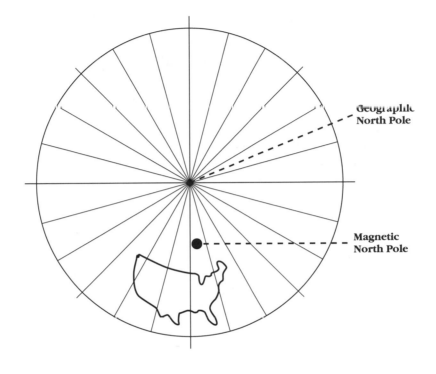

Geographic North Pole

Magnetic North Pole

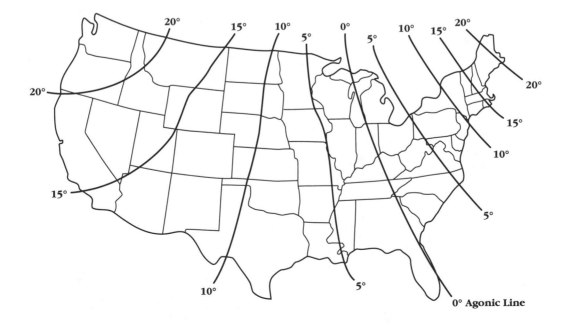

Subtract
Easterly Variation

Add
Westerly Variation

20° 15° 10° 5° 0° 5° 10° 15° 20°

20°

20°

15°

15°

10°

15°

5°

10° 5° 0° Agonic Line

ACTIVITY
2

ROSES

Overview

The compass rose is introduced and students learn that navigation in the air follows essentially the same process as navigating on the ground. They learn that degrees are a basic unit of navigation, and they explore the various patterns and mathematical relationships in the degree measures on a compass rose. They use a circular protractor to interpret and to draw angles representing compass headings for several courses.

Purpose. Students begin to understand the processes used when navigating in the air and appreciate the similarities between navigating on land and in the air. They recognize the importance of angle measurement to convey and determine one's position and direction in navigation.

Time. One to two 40- to 50-minute periods.

Materials. *For each student:*

◆ Student Sheets 2.1–2.3

◆ Circular protractor

◆ Straightedge

For each group of students:

◆ City map

For the teacher:

◆ Transparencies of Student Sheets 2.1–2.3 (optional)

◆ Transparency Master 2.4

◆ Transparency pen

Getting Ready

1. Locate city maps and straightedges.
2. Locate circular protractors. See Resources List (page xiv).
3. Duplicate Student Sheets 2.1–2.3.
4. Prepare Transparency Master 2.4 and locate a transparency pen.
5. Prepare transparencies of Student Sheets 2.1–2.3 (optional).

Background Information

A compass rose oriented toward the north is printed on every map or chart for determining direction. This symbol can be as simple as a single arrow pointing north, or it may be a complete circle divided into compass points and perhaps indicate degree markings from 0°–360°. Compass points mark the cardinal directions of north, south, east, and west and the intercardinal directions of northwest, northeast, southwest, and southeast as well as the intermediate directions NNE, ENE, SSE, and so on. See Transparency Master 2.4.

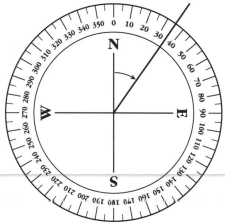

In navigation, the compass heading is expressed as an angle in degrees from 000° to 360°. Direction is always expressed in three digits and read clockwise from true north. A direction 5° northeast is expressed as 005°, and a direction 35° northeast is expressed as 035°. True north may be considered as either 000° or 360° depending on the situation.

Since an angle is often used to show the direction or course to travel, circular protractors similar to the one pictured can be used to measure the compass heading. Circular protractors with 3-inch diameters can be purchased from the C-Thru Ruler Company (see Resources List, page xiv).

Student Sheet 2.1 introduces the compass rose, and Student Sheet 2.2 helps students become familiar with its navigational uses. Students will determine that compass headings greater than 000° and less than 180° are considered easterly directions. Introducing the intercardinal directions allows for headings between 000° and 090° to represent a northeast direction, while headings between 090° and 180° represent a southeast direction. Due east is 090°. While it is possible to determine decimal compass headings, in actuality pilots calculate them to the nearest whole degree.

Students will discover a mathematical relationship between a compass heading in one direction and the compass heading for returning in the opposite direction. By drawing course-lines from the center of the compass rose provided on Student Sheet 2.2 and extending them in the opposite direction as illustrated, they will notice that the return direction is always 180° greater or less than the initial direction. For example, a compass heading of 060° has a northeast direction and the opposite direction is south-west with a compass heading of 240°.

Compass Heading	Direction	Opposite Direction	Opposite Compass Heading
060°	Northeast	Southwest	240°

Student Sheet 2.3 provides experience in relating navigating on land to navigating in the air. Students will rewrite the directions to travel to school by car in terms of compass headings and discover the majority of compass headings are multiples of 90° due to the rectangular layout of the roads. They will then develop directions to fly to school and discover that the directions are much more simple and direct.

The History Link "Wright Brothers" may be used at any time during this unit to stimulate student interest.

Presenting the Activity

Compass Rose. Divide your class into small working groups. Tell students that when giving directions, people often say things such as, ". . . a few miles north of here," and "That's on the east side of town." Ask students:

◆ What do the words *north* and *east* refer to? (Discuss compass directions and how and why they are used.)

◆ Is there is a symbol on the map that indicates direction?

Once students conclude that north is shown, discuss the importance of the symbol called a compass rose. Have students decide what direction the streets and avenues seem to run on a city map. Discuss the number of degrees in a right-hand turn on a city map.

Hand out Student Sheet 2.1. As students are writing their descriptions of the compass rose, hand out the circular protractors so they can complete the sheet.

Explain that to navigate an airplane, a pilot uses some of the same tools and methods involved in traveling by land. A pilot's map is called a chart. A map shows roadways, an aeronautical chart shows airways. If possible, refer to an aeronautical sectional chart displayed in the classroom. When pilots fly, they give directions in degrees. Pilots use the degrees on a circle, called compass headings, to determine their direction. The number of degrees tells them how far to turn clockwise from north.

Compass rose symbols are often more detailed on charts than they are on maps. Display Transparency Master 2.4 to show examples of other compass roses. Ask the class to compare the two patterns and to compare them with the compass rose on their city map. Tell students the circular protractor will be used for measuring direction throughout this unit.

On the second compass rose on Transparency Master 2.4, use a transparency pen to draw angles with respect to true north that represent various compass headings, such as 025°, 190°, and 230°. Explain that direction is always read clockwise from true north. Ask groups to decide how to indicate a course heading of 310° on the transparency. Have them decide if this plane is flying north, south, east, or west. Demonstrate the result based on their input.

Compass Headings. Hand out Student Sheet 2.2. Emphasize that this activity will familiarize them with the compass rose—a necessary navigational tool for a pilot.

As students complete the first page of Student Sheet 2.2, discuss with each group how the cardinal directions of north, south, east, and west divide the compass into quadrants. Clarify the concepts of *between, less than,* and *greater than.* If students suggest that an easterly direction is between 001° and 179°, ask them about 179.5°, 179.8°, and 179.9°. At the same time, you may want to tell students that pilots give directions to the nearest whole degree.

At the completion of Student Sheet 2.2, have several students present and discuss their methods for calculating the compass heading for a return flight in the opposite direction. Use Transparency Master 2.4 to demonstrate this concept. Point out how any course-line and its extension in the opposite direction divides the compass rose into two congruent protractors, each equivalent to 180°.

Flight School. Have students review how they travel by car to school or have them refer to the directions they wrote on Student Sheet 1.1. Hand out Student Sheet 2.3 and have the students rewrite the directions in terms of compass headings. Discuss the results as a class. Point out that most of the compass headings will be multiples of 90°—90° or 270°. Ask students why they think this is so. Students should realize that this predominance of multiples of 90° is due to the predominance of right turns on the roads.

Have the students complete Students Sheet 2.3. With the class, compare and contrast the directions for travel by car and by plane.

Discussion Questions

1. Why and when are the cardinal and intercardinal directions on a compass rose useful?

2. Why is the return flight in the opposite direction always 180° different?

3. What are the similarities and differences between a compass rose, a circular protractor, and a magnetic compass?

4. Why do you suppose compass headings are always written with three digits?

Assessment Strategies

1. A pilot is traveling on a compass heading of 315°. What course heading should the pilot follow for the return flight? Explain.

2. If you know the specific compass heading a plane is flying, can you determine the intercardinal direction it must be flying? Explain.

3. Write the directions for "flying" from your home to school, then to another school for a ball game, and finally back home.

Wright Brothers

Fifty-seven . . . fifty-eight . . . fifty-nine! Fifty-nine seconds doing what most people thought was absurdly impossible—flying. But Wilbur Wright had done it in *Flyer*, the first gasoline-powered flying machine. And his younger brother, Orville, had made the very first flight of the day. He flew for 12 seconds and traveled 120 feet (37 meters).

The Wright brothers made three flights in their flying machine on that day, December 17, 1903, near Kitty Hawk, North Carolina. Their success in controlling and staying airborne in an airplane that was heavier than air was a great achievement. It would take five years, however, before the rest of the world began to realize how important their achievement was.

Wilber and Orville had worked hard on their flying machine and on their aviation skills. For years they tested gliders, studied aeronautics, and even built a wind tunnel in their shop so they could experiment with model wings.

After their successful flights near Kitty Hawk, the Wright brothers continued to improve the construction of their flying machine. By 1908, the United States military and nations in Europe were enthusiastic about the possibilities of an airplane that could carry passengers and stay in the air for over an hour. Other inventors were also doing amazing feats with their flying machines, and aviation progressed quickly.

Aviation progressed so quickly, in fact, that just thirty years after the Wright brothers' success with *Flyer*, the Boeing 247D was launched. This was the first modern airliner, and it carried passengers across the entire United States in under twenty hours.

Compass Rose

1. A picture of a compass rose is given below. With your group, study and discuss it. Why do you think it is called a compass rose?

2. Write a description of the compass rose that someone who cannot see it will understand.

3. How does the compass rose compare to a circular protractor?

4. A compass rose always appears somewhere on a map. Find the compass rose on your map and compare it to the compass rose above.

Compass Headings

1. Degrees are the units of measure you used in navigating the compass walks. Degrees are also the units of measure used to give the direction in which an airplane is flying. In aviation, compass headings are always written as three-digit numbers. A compass heading of eight degrees is written 008°. A compass heading of twenty-five degrees is written _____, and a compass heading of one hundred thirty-five degrees is written _____.

2. According to the compass rose, a plane traveling due east is on a compass heading of _____ degrees.

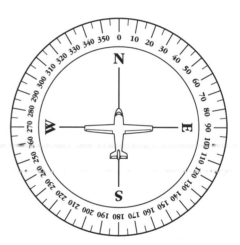

3. To head west in the opposite direction, a pilot flies a course that has a compass heading of _____ degrees.

4. A plane flying due north has a compass heading of _____ degrees; whereas a plane flying due south has a compass heading of _____ degrees.

5. The directions of _____, _____, _____, and _____ divide the compass rose into four equal parts, called quadrants. These are the cardinal directions.

6. A compass heading of 310° is both _____ and _____. Therefore the direction of this course is _____.

7. Beginning with the northeast intercardinal direction and continuing clockwise on the compass, list the intercardinal directions represented by the four quadrants on the compass rose. Give two possible compass headings within each intercardinal direction.

Intercardinal Direction	Possible Compass Headings

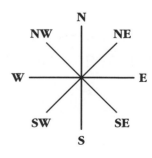

Compass Headings

8. From the center of the compass rose, draw a course-line with a 010° compass heading. A 010° compass heading represents a northeast direction. Extend this same course-line in the opposite direction to describe a southwest heading of _____ degrees.

9. Use the indicated compass headings to draw course-lines on the compass rose. Extend each course-line to determine the compass heading in the opposite direction.

Compass Heading	Direction	Opposite Direction	Opposite Compass Heading
060°			
100°			
175°			
240°			
270°			
310°			
335°			

10. If you are given a compass heading, how could you determine the compass heading in the opposite direction without drawing the course-line?

11. Use a circular protractor to determine the compass headings for the courses shown below.

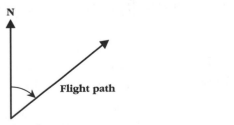

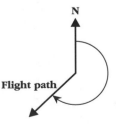

12. With a straightedge and a circular protractor, draw angles to represent courses for compass headings of 025°, 155°, and 300°.

Flight School

1. On Student Sheet 1.1, you determined how to travel by car between your school and _____ Park.

   a. Using a compass rose or a circular protractor, rewrite these directions using compass headings. Remember that a compass heading always reads clockwise from due north.

   b. What do you notice about the compass headings? Explain.

2. Superman is going to fly from your school to this park.
   a. What is the compass heading for his flight to the park?

   b. Estimate the distance of the flight.

   c. What is the compass heading for his return flight to school?

3. Locate another school on the map. It is _____. Write directions for Wonderwoman to fly from your school to the other school and back to your school.

Flight School

4. Write directions for you to fly from home to school.

   a. What is the compass heading?

   b. Estimate the distance of your flight.

   c. What is the difference between the distance by car and the distance by air?

   d. What is the compass heading for going home from school?

5. Write directions for you to fly home from school, with a stop at _____ to get a drink of water.

6. Sketch the flight path used in (5), including the course headings.

Compass Roses

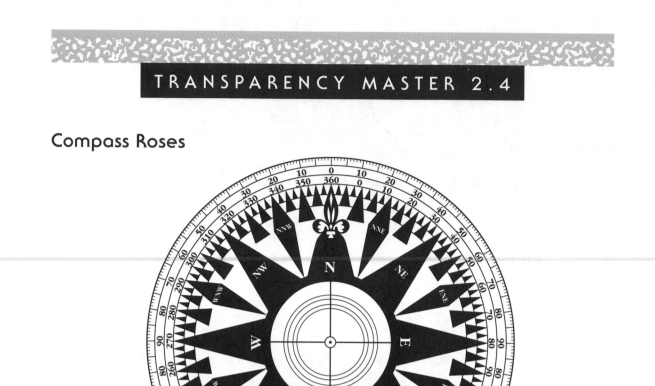

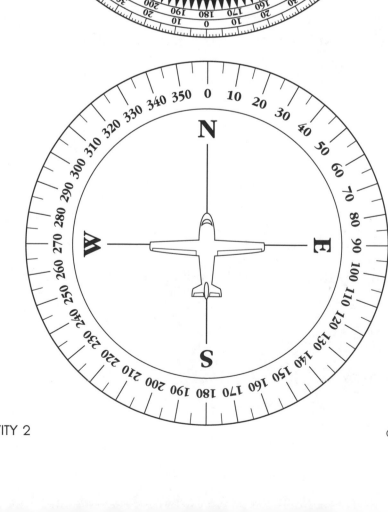

ACTIVITY
3

DESTINATION, DIRECTION, AND DISTANCE

Overview

Students learn about the three basics of navigation: destination, direction, and distance. Students use state maps to investigate the process involved in charting and navigating an aeronautical course. They draw course-lines, determine directions, and calculate distances.

Purpose. Students realize the process involved in charting and navigating an aeronautical course and acquire skill with circular protractors and scaling procedures.

Time. One to two 40- to 50-minute periods.

Materials. *For each student:*

◆ Student Sheets 3.1–3.4
◆ Directions for traveling by car (prepared by the teacher)

For each group of students:

◆ Laminated state map (1 per pair of students)
◆ Sponge or paper towel
◆ Circular protractor (1 per pair of students)
◆ Centimeter ruler (1 per pair of students)
◆ Transparency pen
◆ At least one calculator, a spray bottle of water, and a meter stick

For the teacher:

◆ Transparency of a state map
◆ Transparency pen
◆ Transparencies of Student Sheets 3.1–3.4 (optional)
◆ Aeronautical sectional chart (optional)
◆ Globe or Transparency Master 3.5

Getting Ready

1. Locate and laminate state maps.
2. Locate protractors, rulers, sponges, transparency pens, calculators, spray bottles, meter sticks, and a globe (optional).
3. Write a set of directions for traveling by car from your city to a familiar location.
4 Duplicate Student Sheets 3.1–3.4.
5. Display aeronautical sectional chart (optional).
6. Prepare transparency of the state map (can be a simple rendition).
7. Prepare transparencies of Student Sheets 3.1–3.3 (optional).
8. Locate globe or prepare Transparency Master 3.5 (optional).

Background Information

Using a chart, a pilot can determine headings to various locations as well as distances to those locations. State maps adequately provide the necessary information for charting accurate courses. They are substituted for charts to draw and to measure course-lines between airports, as well as to chart a flight plan. State maps may or may not include lines of latitude or longitude, but this information is not necessary for charting a visual flight course.

On all charts, north is a unique direction everywhere on the chart, and on almost all charts north is straight up, toward the top of the page. Finding the direction from one point to another means finding out how many degrees to rotate clockwise from north in order to face the desired direction.

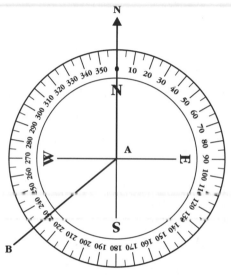

One way to do this is to draw a line north from the starting point, A, and a course-line that runs from the starting point to the destination, B. Then use a circular protractor to measure the angle between the course-line and north. Traveling from A to B as illustrated requires a compass heading of 230°. This is the method used on Student Sheet 3.2 to determine direction without the use of latitude and longitude lines.

The Interest Link "Parallels and Meridians" can be used at any time during this activity to help students understand how pilots can use latitude and longitude in navigation. Transparency Master 3.5 is to be used with this Interest Link.

On opposite sides of state maps, there are often equally-spaced corresponding sets of numbers. Carefully connecting those across the top of the map with those across the bottom results in a series of north facing lines representing meridians. By drawing several of these parallel lines, students can actually measure the direction of a course with respect to the meridians.

Student Sheet 3.1 gives students an opportunity to explore a state map. Students should work in pairs, and each pair needs a map. King of the Road Maps (see Resources List, p. xiv) will sell state maps at $0.66 each for orders of at least 100. If you call them two to four months in advance, they may have the maps you require in old stock. These are free. Try not to submit your request during the summer, because that is their busiest time. Laminating the maps makes them reusable for subsequent classes, and students can use transparency pens on this working surface to easily alter, adjust, or emphasize course-lines.

Student Sheet 3.2 provides an introduction to course-lines and the basics for determining flight plans—location, destination, direction, and distance. It is important that all course-lines plotted on a chart be properly labeled. The use of standardized methods ensures that the plot will mean the same thing to others as it does to the navigator who makes it. The principle rules for labeling a course-line are:

1. Label the course-line immediately after drawing it.

2. Label a direction with the letter C followed by the true course in degrees. Place it above an east/west line and to the right of a north/south line. Use an arrow to indicate direction of motion.

3. Label distance with the letter D followed by the distance in nautical or statute miles, usually to the nearest tenth of a mile. Place this below an east/west course-line or to the left of a north/south course-line.

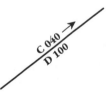

The basic elements in determining an aeronautical course are:

1. Location. On the chart, the pilot locates the known starting point, usually an airport.

2. Destination. The pilot then locates the intended destination, also an airport.

3. Direction. A line is drawn from one to the other, called a course-line. Using a compass rose and a circular protractor, the pilot determines the compass heading and labels it.

4. Distance. The pilot measures the length of this line, uses the appropriate scale to find the distance from the starting point to the destination, and labels it.

Because pilots generally fly from airport to airport, it is important to note the locations of airports throughout the state. There are more than

16,000 airports in the United States, although not all of these are marked on regular state maps.

One way to calculate the distance between your current location and intended destination on a chart is to measure the length of the course-line and use the indicated scale to convert to miles. On most state maps, the scale is in inches. Since rates in this country are computed in miles per hour, this module uses inches and miles. If you prefer to emphasize the metric system, conversion to meters could be done.

As an example, the scale on one map used 1.0 inch to represent 14.9 miles. A course-line between airports near Seattle and Richland measures 11.2 inches. The following proportion can be solved to determine the distance in miles.

$$\frac{1}{14.9} = \frac{11.2}{x}$$

$$x = 166.9 \text{ miles}$$

Typically, a pilot uses dividers or a ruler to mark off 10-mile sections along a course-line for convenience and quick reference. Since all sectional charts are scaled with 1 inch equivalent to approximately 8 miles, special plotting rulers are available which automatically convert the length of a course-line to both statute and nautical miles.

Aeronautical distances are generally recorded in nautical miles. Navigators on the sea and in the air find the use of nautical miles for distance measurement convenient because a nautical mile is about 6,000 feet and is also equivalent to 1 minute of latitude. Mileage scales for both nautical and statute miles are on aeronautical charts and plotters. At this time, the Federal Aviation Administration mixes statute and nautical measurements indiscriminately. This unit does not develop the concept of a nautical mile. Conversions and information are based on statute miles only.

You may consider showing some of the course-lines generated by Student Sheet 3.2 directly on the aeronautical chart, if you have one displayed in the classroom, using push-pins and yarn. This will give a visual comparison between students' state map course-lines and the same courses on an actual aeronautical chart.

The Technology Link "Flying Machines" can be used at any time during this activity to stimulate student interest.

Presenting the Activity

State Maps. Divide your class into pairs. Put up the transparency of the state map. You can make this by drawing the rough shape of the map and giving the location of two or three cities. Guide students through the procedure for determining a course-line, and then go over the principles of labeling it.

Distribute the state maps, rulers, circular protractors, and Student Sheet 3.1. When students are done, discuss the three basics of navigation: destination, distance to travel, and direction. Explain that all navigation begins with a starting point, commonly referred to as location. From there, a pilot uses mathematics to calculate the direction and distance to travel to arrive at the destination.

3-D. Divide your class into small working groups. Distribute sponges, spray bottles, transparency pens, meter sticks, calculators, and Student Sheet 3.2. Explain that a state map provides enough information to accurately chart a flight. Most visual flight pilots travel with both a state map and the appropriate sectional chart. Inform the groups that they are going to learn how to chart an aeronautical course. After they work the first exercise, review the basic process:

1. Location. On a chart, the pilot locates the known starting point, usually an airport.

2. Destination. The pilot then locates the intended destination, also an airport.

3. Direction. A line is drawn from one to the other, called a course-line. Using a compass rose and a circular protractor, the pilot determines the compass heading. Ensure that the students know north is always the starting point for measuring direction, and that they know how to correctly place the circular protractor with its center aligned on the airport representing the starting point.

4. Distance. The pilot measures the length of this line and uses the map scale to find the distance from the starting point to the destination.

You may choose to have a group demonstrate the above process on the transparency representation of the state map.

Have the students complete Student Sheet 3.2. Point out that at any time, course-lines can be altered or removed from the laminated surface of the map by spraying water onto a sponge and wiping the area clean.

Round Trips. As each group completes Student Sheet 3.2, discuss the process with them. As they are ready, give them Student Sheets 3.3 and 3.4, which extend the work to include the return trip. At the end of the period, remind students to clean off their state maps.

Discussion Questions

1. How many lines can you draw on a map from one specific location that point toward true north?

2. If you select fifty airports on a map and draw lines extending north from each one, what would you notice about all these lines?

3. When would the distance to travel between two cities by land be greater than the distance to travel by air? be equal to the distance by air? be less than the distance by air?

4. To navigate by air, what do you need to consider besides the destination, direction, and distance? (One answer would be the wind conditions.)

Assessment Strategies

1. If you were to fly from your city to the state capitol, what course heading would you use?

2. Read the Interest Link "Parallels and Meridians." Locate three meridians on your map or draw in lines to represent them. From an airport near your city, extend a 060° course-line that intersects each meridian. Measure the direction of this course-line at the intersection of each meridian. What do you notice about the results? What can you conclude?

3. Pick two cities in your state that you have never visited. Chart a trip to visit them, returning home at the end of the trip. Give the information in both prose and table formats.

Parallels and Meridians

Imagine you could take the earth shown below and cut it in half along the equator. What you would cut through is one of the lines of latitude. You can see the lines of latitude on the diagram below. They are complete circles around the earth that are parallel to each other. You can see the entire circle of the line of latitude surrounding the north pole. These lines are also called *parallels*. Parallels do not all have the same circumference. Think about how big each circle of the earth would be if you sliced it along the parallels as if you were making onion rings.

Now imagine cutting the earth into thin wedges, somewhat like orange segments. The lines that divide the earth into wedges are called lines of longitude. They extend from pole to pole. These lines are also called *meridians*. Meridians are all the same length.

Another way to determine compass headings involves the meridians. On an aeronautical chart, meridians, by definition, always point north. Since the meridian is a line running north and south, a pilot can use this line to determine which direction to fly. The pilot would draw the course-line and measure the angle where the course-line intersects the meridian.

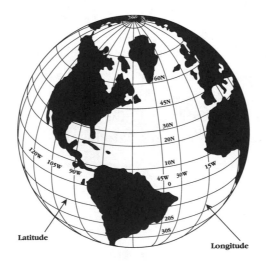

Flying Machines

Someday you may look up and notice what at first seems like a plane zooming overhead. But wait! It doesn't look like a whole plane, it looks like just a wing—a flying wing! In fact, that is what it is. Although this plane has not yet been built, its designer has shown through models how the wing can fly. In theory, the flying wing would be a more efficient, faster flying machine than planes we have today.

The flying wing is just one example of how flying machines may change in the future. Engineers and designers are constantly searching for ways to improve our travel through the skies.

The military already has planes that look very futuristic. One stealth bomber, called the F-117A, which has everything from radar deflection to high tech infrared scopes, looks more like a sleek, black boomerang than a plane.

In 1986, one inventor showed how his futuristic plane could soar around the world without stopping or refueling. From the back, the plane looked like a long, horizontal toothpick with two propellers. From the tip of one wing to the other, the plane was 111 feet wide!

Researchers are already working on making miniature planes that can turn into "cars" for road travel. You would be able to either drive or fly to work, school, or the store!

Already, there is a plane that flies on solar energy, a jet that lifts off the ground like a helicopter, and an ultra-light plane that packs into a large suitcase.

What do you think airplanes of the future will look like or do? Write a paragraph describing what you imagine.

State Maps

1. Locate your city on a state map.

2. Is your city located in the north, south, east, or west part of the state? Explain.

3. Using the state map, follow the written directions given to you. They begin at your city and end at a familiar location.

   a. Describe the final destination.

   b. How did you know the destination?

   c. What is the distance scale of your map?

   d. Estimate the distance of your trip.

4. Using a circular protractor, determine the course heading you would need to fly this route, and chart a course-line between the location (starting point) and the destination (ending point). Write the course heading on top of the line and write the distance below it.

5. Does your city have an airport?

   a. If it does, is it marked on the map? Explain.

   b. If not, locate the nearest airport.

6. Pick a city in your state you would like to visit. Use the circular protractor to determine the compass heading you would use to fly from your city to that city. Chart the course-line and sketch it below.

3-D

A pilot always begins a flight from a known point on a chart or a map. From that point, the course to fly is determined by the three *D's*: destination, direction, and distance.

1. Follow these steps to chart an aeronautical course between two airports:
   a. Find an airport near your city on a state map and mark its location with a point.
   b. Draw a line from the point that represents the direction north. Use the indicator for north on your map to help you.
   c. Choose another airport near a different city on the state map as your destination.
   d. Draw a course-line connecting the two airports.
   e. Measure the angle the course-line makes with true north to determine your compass heading (or the direction of flight).
   f. Use the mileage scale on the state map to calculate the distance in miles along the course-line from your location to your destination.
   Location (starting point):
   Destination (ending point):
   Direction (compass heading):
   Distance:

   Sometimes, this is all that you need to chart an aeronautical course.

2. Locate some place of interest that is about 100 miles from the airport near your city. Draw a course-line and determine the direction.
   Location:
   Destination:
   Direction:
   Distance:

3. If you leave this airport on a compass heading of 40° and travel for 150 miles, where are you? What compass heading should you follow to return home?
   Location:
   Destination:
   Direction:
   Distance:

Round Trips

1. Pick an airport near your home and another that is on the opposite side of the state. Draw a course-line to fly from one airport to the other. Determine the distance and the directions to fly there and back.

	Departing	Returning
Location		
Destination		
Direction		
Distance		

2. Pick two places you would like to visit in the state. Draw course-lines to fly to the first place, then to the second, and then to return home. Each part of your trip is called a "leg."

	First Leg	Second Leg	Third Leg
Location			
Destination			
Direction			
Distance			

3. As a group, plan a trip, giving the starting location with the direction and distance to each stop. Only fill in the places marked with a •. Exchange papers with another group. Follow their directions to determine the destinations and complete their table. Exchange papers again and determine if both groups flew to the intended destinations.

	First Leg	Second Leg	Third Leg
Location	•		
Destination			
Direction	•	•	•
Distance	•	•	•

Charting Courses

1. Locate three other airports on your state map. Chart a 40° course-line from each airport. Extend the course-lines for at least 100 miles. How are the three course-lines related?

2. How many 40° course-lines are there on this map?

3. If you and a friend fly at 120° course headings from two different airports within the state, where will you intersect each other?

4. Discuss as a group the findings from questions 1 through 3 and their importance to aviation. Summarize the group's consensus below.

Globe

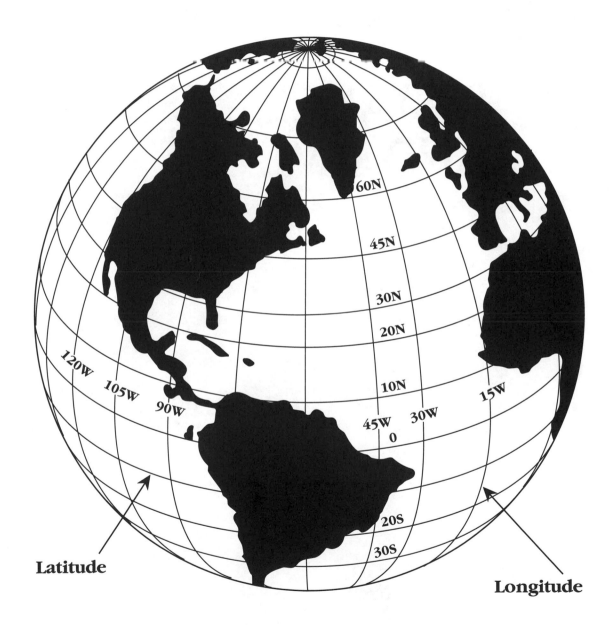

ACTIVITY
4

DISTANCE, SPEED, AND TIME

Overview

While students continue to chart courses between airports on a state map, they discover relationships among distance, speed, and time. Students develop and apply a formula for the relationships. They come to understand the importance of these variables in preparing a flight plan.

Purpose. Students begin to understand the relationships among distance, speed, and time as they experience their use in developing flight plans.

Time. One to two 40- to 50-minute periods.

Materials. *For each student:*

◆ Student Sheets 4.1–4.3

For each group of two students:

◆ Laminated state map
◆ Sponge or paper towel
◆ Circular protractor
◆ Ruler
◆ Transparency pen
◆ Calculator
◆ Spray bottle of water
◆ Meter stick

For the teacher:

◆ Transparencies of Student Sheets 4.1–4.3 and a transparency pen (optional)

Getting Ready

1. Locate laminated state maps, sponges, circular protractors, rulers, transparency pens, calculators, spray bottles, and meter sticks.
2. Duplicate Student Sheets 4.1–4.3.
3. Fill spray bottles with water.
4. Prepare transparencies of Student Sheets 4.1–4.3 and locate a transparency pen (optional).

Background Information

Throughout all navigation, a pilot is confronted with problems involving distance, speed, and time. There are several ways to solve these problems, and it doesn't matter which way a pilot chooses. Most pilots find it convenient to use an aeronautical converter to solve distance (D), speed (S), and time (T) problems. Ground school training emphasizes the importance of being able to solve these types of rate problems quickly and accurately without any equipment.

A rate contains the words *per, for each,* or some other synonym. When used in an expression, a horizontal bar means "per." For example,

$$250 \text{ miles per hour} = 250 \, \frac{\text{miles}}{\text{hour}}$$

When a rate is multiplied by another quantity, the units are also multiplied. The unit of the product is the product of units. The units are multiplied like fractions. For example,

$$250 \, \frac{\text{miles}}{\text{hour}} \times 6 \text{ hours} = 1,500 \text{ miles}$$

Therefore, a plane traveling 250 miles per hour for 6 hours travels 1,500 miles.

Student Sheet 4.1 provides experiences that lead students to discover the following relationships:

$$S \times T = D \quad \text{and} \quad \frac{D}{T} = S \quad \text{and} \quad \frac{D}{S} = T$$

These relationships can then be applied to solve for distance, speed, or time. Three situations and methods of solution using these ideas are presented here:

1. A plane flies 145 miles per hour for 3 hours. How far does it go?

$$
\begin{aligned}
D &= S \times T \\
D &= 145 \, \frac{\text{miles}}{\text{hour}} \times 3 \text{ hours} \\
&= 145 \text{ miles} \times 3 \\
&= 435 \text{ miles}
\end{aligned}
$$

The plane travels 435 miles.

2. A plane flies 600 miles in 3 hours. What is its average speed?

$$S = \frac{D}{T}$$

$$S = \frac{600 \text{ miles}}{3 \text{ hours}}$$

$$S = 200 \frac{\text{miles}}{\text{hour}}$$

$$S = 200 \text{ miles per hour}$$

3. If a plane flies 900 miles at a speed of 150 miles per hour, then how long is the flight?

$$T = \frac{D}{S}$$

$$T = \frac{900 \text{ miles}}{\frac{150 \text{ miles}}{1 \text{ hour}}}$$

$$T = \frac{900 \text{ miles}}{1} \times \frac{1 \text{ hour}}{150 \text{ miles}}$$

$$T = 6 \text{ hours}$$

In this example, related facts are used to convert division into an equivalent multiplication problem using the reciprocal.

Student Sheets 4.2 and 4.3 present opportunities for students to use these relationships in dealing with typical aviation situations.

The Interest Link "How to Become a Pilot" and the Career Link "Susan Darcy" can be used at any time during this activity to stimulate student interest.

Presenting the Activity

D, S, and T. Divide your class into pairs. Tell them pilots know the distance they have flown by knowing both the time they have been flying and their airspeed. Speed is a rate. Ask students to discuss in their pairs what they think a rate is and to give some other examples. List several on the board or overhead projector. You might include

◆ 36 passengers per flight

◆ 8 gallons of fuel per hour (the average a Cessna 172 consumes)

◆ 34 inches of rain per year (average rainfall in Seattle)

Suggest that a quantity is a rate when it includes the words *per* or *for each*. In a mathematical expression, a fraction bar can be used to mean "per." In fraction form, 600 miles per hour becomes $600\,\frac{\text{miles}}{\text{hour}}$. In one hour this plane will fly 600 miles. Ask students how far the plane will fly in two hours. Elicit from them how multiplication gives the expected result.

$$600\,\frac{\text{miles}}{\text{hour}} \times 2 \text{ hours} = 1{,}200 \text{ miles}$$

Elicit how the units in the above multiplication work like factors in fractions. The unit hour in the denominator cancels the unit hour on the right. The unit that remains is miles.

Pass out Student Sheet 4.1 and the calculators. Mention that a pilot must always be able to solve problems involving distance, speed, and time quickly and accurately. As students complete each problem, they should discuss their solutions and responses within their groups.

Discuss question 10 with the class to solidify their understanding of how to solve for distance, speed, and time when two of those quantities are known. Elicit that multiplication and division provide us with related facts. For example:

$$\text{Since } 3 \times 4 = 12, \text{ then } \frac{12}{3} = 4 \text{ and } \frac{12}{4} = 3$$

$$\text{therefore, if } S \times T = D, \text{ then } \frac{D}{S} = T \text{ and } \frac{D}{T} = S$$

Remind students to refer back to simpler and more obvious problems, if the situation or the numbers become complicated.

More *D, S,* and *T.* When the class is familiar with the relationships among distance, speed, and time, hand out Student Sheet 4.2. Have the students complete the page. While they are working, talk with each pair of students about question 10 on Student Sheet 4.1. Make sure they comprehend that there are three different expressions for the relationship among distance, speed, and time. Pass out Student Sheet 4.3. The last problem is a preamble to Activity 5, in which they develop a cross-country flight plan.

Discussion Questions

1. Why must pilots know how to solve rate problems? Who else needs these skills?

2. The distance a person travels is a function of time. What does this statement mean?

3. There are three expressions for the relationship among distance, speed, and time. Is there one you prefer? Explain.

4. Explain how to convert decimal parts of hours to minutes.

Assessment Strategies

1. Complete the tables below and prepare a graph of time versus distance for both Table A and Table B on the same set of axes.

Table A

Speed (mph)	Time (hours)	Distance (miles)
100	0.00	
100	2.50	
100	4.00	
100	5.25	
100	6.50	

Table B

Speed (mph)	Time (hours)	Distance (miles)
250		0.0
250		125.0
250		562.5
250		875.0
250		1,000.0

What do you notice? Describe your results.

2. What happens to the distance if the speed and the time are both doubled? Explain in writing, using examples to document your argument.

3. Work in groups to design and develop a process to determine what happens to the distance if the rate is doubled and the time is halved.

How to Become a Pilot

You climb into the cockpit of the jetliner. This is your first time serving as a captain for a major airline. You had worked on a commuter airline until you recorded the 2,500 hours of flight time needed to apply for this job. You have already carefully planned the flight, carefully inspected the engine and instruments, and made sure the baggage was loaded correctly.

As the copilot watches the instrument panel, you taxi to the runway and radio the tower. You know the speed the aircraft needs to reach in order to take off by calculating the altitude of the airport, wind speed, temperature, weight of the plane, and other factors. As you zoom down the runway, the copilot tells you the moment the plane reaches takeoff speed. You pull back on the controls and lift the nose of the plane.

To become a pilot, you first got your bachelor's degree in aviation flight technology. You received your pilot's license with certificates for commercial instrument, multi-engine, and flight ratings. You also had to pass a strict physical exam to work as a professional pilot.

There are many advantages to your job. The pay is excellent. As a captain for a major airline, you could earn over $100,000 a year after some work experience. You and your family also receive free air travel to many places in the world.

However, there are some disadvantages. Planes leave at all hours of the day and night. Since you are a newer employee, you do not get to choose your flights on the schedule. So you often work irregular hours. Sometimes you work more than twelve hours a day and then have nine hours off in whatever city your last flight ended.

Susan Darcy

Susan Darcy started at Boeing as an engineer's assistant, but what she really wanted was to fly. She began taking flying lessons that cost almost her entire paycheck. Soon she earned her instructor's license and worked as an instructor to accumulate flight hours. While doing all this, she completed a degree in aeronautical and astronautical engineering at the University of Washington. In November, 1984, she set a goal: she wanted a career as a professional pilot within one year. On October 31, 1985, she was hired as Boeing's first female test pilot!

Darcy says the best part of her job is that she gets paid to do what she loves. Her workdays average 12 hours and can begin at 7:00 A.M. or end at 3:00 A.M. Planes are tested in all kinds of weather and situations, and Darcy never knows exactly what the next day will be like. Some days she flies as captain, some days as co-captain. She is required to fly all the Boeing models: the 737, 747-400, 757, and 767. She gets to fly everything! She trains pilots and delivers planes in places like China, Russia, Australia, Hong Kong, and Germany.

Darcy says the basic idea behind flying a Cessna 172 and a Boeing 747 is the same; there's just an 875,000-pound difference!

Susan Darcy (right) with fellow pilot Leon Robert.

D, S, and T

All navigation involves three factors: distance (*D*), speed (*S*), and time (*T*).
A pilot will know two of these and need to figure out the third.

1. A plane flying at 130 miles per hour (mph) will fly 130 miles in one hour.

   a. How far will this plane fly in half an hour? _____

   b. How far will this plane fly in two hours? _____

2. Complete the table to determine the distances flown from Olympia,
   Washington, to these other cities.

Destination	Speed	Time	Distance
Spokane, WA	135 mph	2.0 hours	
Richland/Pasco, WA	144 mph	1.25 hours	
Seattle/Tacoma, WA	130 mph	0.4 hours	
Portland, OR	132 mph	0.75 hours	

3. If you know the speed and time, how can you calculate the distance?

4. A plane flying 150 miles per hour travels a distance of 75 miles. What is the
   flight time? Explain.

5. Complete this table to find the flight times from Salem, Oregon, to the various
   locations.

Destination	Speed	Time	Distance
Eugene, OR	130 mph		65 miles
Bend, OR	132 mph		99 miles
Pendleton, OR	136 mph		170 miles
Yakima, WA	152 mph		190 miles

D, S, and T

6. If you know the speed and distance, how can you calculate the time?

7. If you fly 1,000 miles in 4 hours, then you traveled _____ miles in 1 hour. What is your airspeed? Explain.

8. Complete the following table to determine the airspeeds for planes flying from Sacramento, California, to the following cities.

Destination	Speed	Time	Distance
Reno, NV		0.75 hours	99 miles
San Francisco, CA		0.6 hours	81 miles
Bakersfield, CA		1.5 hours	201 miles
Los Angeles, CA		2.5 hours	360 miles

9. If you know the time and distance, how can you calculate the speed? Explain.

10. **Distance, Speed, and Time.** If you know any two of these, explain how you can find the third.

More *D, S,* and *T*

1. Work the three problems below and then discuss with your group how they are related.

   a. A plane flies 450 miles in three hours. What is its average speed?

   b. A plane flies 450 miles at a speed of 150 miles per hour. How long is the flight?

   c. A plane flies for three hours at a speed of 150 miles per hour. How far does it go?

2. Discuss with your group how the three questions are related and write a brief statement explaining the relationship.

Using *D, S,* and *T*

1. Calculate the expected airspeed if the course-line on an aeronautical chart measures 1,560 miles, and the flying time allotted is 12 hours.

2. A Cessna 172 has an average speed of approximately 155 miles per hour. You are asked to take it for a test flight 3.5 hours before sunset. What is the farthest possible total distance you can fly the Cessna and be sure to return before dark?

3. At 10:00 A.M. you are 2.5 hours into a 650-mile flight when advancing head winds cut your airspeed in half. If your airspeed at the start of the trip was 130 miles per hour, what is your revised estimated time of arrival (ETA)?

4. As a group, pick two places in the state you would like to visit. Assume you will average 150 miles per hour in your Cessna 172. Develop and record a flight plan. What is the flying time to complete the visits and return home? Give the flying time first in tenths of hours, then convert it to hours and minutes.

ACTIVITY
5

DEAD RECKONING

Overview

Students use dead reckoning to chart an aeronautical course on a state map. They prepare a detailed flight plan to satisfy criteria for a cross-country venture in a Cessna 172 that will involve at least three stops before returning home. Then they examine an aeronautical sectional chart in their groups, locating familiar landmarks and interpreting some of the symbols. They compare their charted courses on state maps with the courses as they would appear on the aeronautical sectional.

Purpose. This activity applies the mathematical concepts and navigational skills developed in the previous activities. Students recognize the similarities and differences between charting a course on a state map versus a comparable aeronautical sectional chart.

Time. One to two 40- to 50-minute periods.

Materials. *For each student:*

◆ Student Sheet 5.1

For each group of two students:

◆ Laminated state map

◆ Sponge or paper towel

◆ Circular protractor

◆ Ruler

◆ Transparency pen

◆ Calculator, spray bottle of water, and a meter stick

◆ Aeronautical sectional chart

For the teacher:

◆ Transparency of Student Sheet 5.1 (optional)

Getting Ready

1. Locate laminated state maps, sponges, circular protractors, rulers, transparency pens, calculators, spray bottles, and meter sticks.

2. Locate aeronautical sectional charts for your area.

3. Duplicate Student Sheet 5.1.

4. Prepare transparency of Student Sheet 5.1 (optional).

5. Fill spray bottles with water.

Background Information

Air navigation is not limited to the actual guiding of an airplane from one place to another—it begins and ends on the ground. This planning phase is called dead reckoning. Dead reckoning is the navigation of a plane solely by means of computations based on airspeed, course headings, and elapsed time. The simplest form of dead reckoning assumes the air is calm.

Student Sheet 5.1 presents specific criteria for students to follow while using dead reckoning to prepare a flight plan for a cross-country journey in a four-seater Cessna 172. A Cessna 172 travels 110–145 knots, which is approximately equivalent to 126–167 miles per hour. They hold up to 40 gallons of fuel and use anywhere from 6–14 gallons per hour. A pilot considers a full tank of fuel to be equivalent to 4.5 hours of flying time.

Using a laminated state map as a chart, students must determine airport locations, course directions, and distances. They incorporate actual departure and arrival times based on use of speed, time, and distance relationships, and they establish rates of fuel consumption.

For this activity, students should work in pairs. The conditions are set for possible flights within Washington State. It may be necessary to creatively alter some of the criteria for successful flight plans in other states. For example, changing the initial departure time and final return time, or increasing the airspeed requirement from 130 miles per hour to 150 miles per hour, may be helpful in a larger state. Keep in mind that some students' proposed flight plans may adhere to the criteria more closely than others. If aspects of their data diverge slightly from the criteria, you may either determine it insignificant, or allow students on an individual basis to negotiate specific modifications in the criteria with you. Completing a flight plan that accurately assesses direction, distance, fuel, and time components is the primary goal. Meeting the contingencies of the activity is a secondary goal.

The most important aspect of a cross-country flight is the aeronautical chart. Three types of charts are available for visual navigation of slow- to medium-speed aircraft. World Aeronautical Charts are printed on a scale of 1:1,000,000. This means that 1 inch on the chart represents 1,000,000 inches on the ground or approximately 16 miles. Sectional charts, which are used for most local- and medium-range cross-country navigation, are on a scale of 1:500,000, or approximately 8 miles per inch.

Sectionals are excellent for visual navigation. They show roads, freeways, railroads, power lines, lakes, rivers, terrain contours, and populated areas. Controlled airspace, military airfields, and public, private, and emergency airports are also shown. It takes 37 sectional charts to cover the continental United States. Terminal Control Area charts (TCAs), with a scale of 1:250,000, or approximately 4 miles per inch, are published for some areas. Locations of TCAs are indicated by a * on the sectional chart index.

It may require more than one aeronautical sectional to cover a specific state. At the very least, portions of the state will be displayed on both sides of a chart. To plot a course between two airports located either on different charts or on opposite sides of a sectional, a pilot will plot and measure a course-line to an intermediary location that is repeated either on the other chart or the reverse side. Another course-line is drawn from the overlapping location to the final destination, and the direction is reassessed. Because of the speed, time, and distance relationship, a pilot knows when he or she will fly over the intermediary position. When it is visually identified, the compass heading will be appropriately altered to complete the flight.

Before departure, a pilot will file a flight plan with the Federal Aviation Agency similar to the format used here and on Student Sheet 5.1. The flight plan below represents a possible scenario for a cross-country journey within Washington State. It is customary to round distances to the nearest tenth of a mile, time to the hundredths of an hour or the nearest minute, and compass headings to the nearest degree.

Flight Plan

Depart Time	Location	Destination	Compass Heading	Distance	Fuel in Tank	Fuel Usage	Flight Time	Arrival Time
9:00 A.M.	Seattle	Clallum Bay	304°	110.3 mi.	40*	8	0.85 h or 51 min	9:51 A.M.
10:06 A.M.	Clallum Bay	Olympia	147°	113.3 mi.	32	8	0.87 h or 52 min	10:58 A.M.
11:45 A.M.	Olympia	Pullman	092°	278.5 mi.	24	18	2.14 h or 2 h 9 min	1:54 P.M.
2:30 P.M.	Pullman	Spokane	338°	64.9 mi.	6	4	0.5 h or 30 min	3:00 P.M.
3:46 P.M.	Spokane	Seattle	266°	226.6 mi.	40*	14	1.74 h or 1 h 45 min	5:31 P.M.

* Indicates a stop for refueling

The flight time indicates the actual time in the air for each leg of the cross country venture. The first leg of the flight measures 7.4 inches on a Washington State map with a scale of 1 inches = ~14.9 miles. This converts to a distance of 110.3 miles. At an airspeed of 130 miles per hour, the computed flight time using T = D/S is .85 hours. Since there are 60 minutes in an hour, the actual flight time in minutes is .85 of 60 or 51 minutes.

Recall that all maps and charts relate to true north, even though there is nothing in the airplane that relates to true north. The magnetic compass indicates the direction to the magnetic north pole which is in Northern Canada. Pilots take the variation between true north and magnetic north into account when filing a flight plan. This information is shown on all aeronautical sectional charts as red, dashed, isogonic lines. Provide appropriate sectionals for students who wish to include magnetic variation in their flight data. Throughout most of Washington State, pilots use the average magnetic variation as –20° to determine their magnetic heading. This unit does not incorporate magnetic north. If it does come up in class, you should discuss this, and give students the option to develop their flight plan using either true or magnetic north.

Compass Heading	Magnetic Variation for Washington	Magnetic Heading
304°	–20°	284°
147°	–20°	127°
092°	–20°	072°
338°	–20°	318°
266°	–20°	246°

The Technology Link "Radar" and the History Link "WASPs" may be used at any time during this activity to stimulate student interest.

Presenting the Activity

The State of Flying. Divide your class into pairs. Explain that to qualify for a private pilot certificate, a student pilot must complete at least one cross-country fight. With input from the class, define a cross-country flight as one that involves several stops throughout the state before returning home. By definition, it requires a great deal of preflight planning and information.

Ask the class what they think this information entails. Their responses should include, but not be limited to, locations of airports near intended destinations, plotting course-lines on a chart, determining compass headings between airports, measuring distances, calculating flight time, as well as finding departure and arrival times. Tell them that pilots refer to this process as dead reckoning: a system of determining where the plane should be on the basis of where it has been. The word *dead* comes from "ded," which is an abbreviation for deduced. *Dead reckoning* is actually *deduced reckoning*.

Discuss how flight time compares to departure and arrival times. Point out that flight time is the amount of time necessary to complete the flight. Ask students:

◆ What information does a pilot need in order to compute flight time? (distance and speed)

◆ What is meant by departure time?

◆ What affects it?

◆ How is arrival time related to departure time?

Establish that departure time is completely independent of flight time; whereas arrival time is dependent upon both the hour of departure and the flight time.

Distribute both pages of Student Sheet 5.1, state maps, sponges, circular protractors, rulers, transparency pens, calculators, spray bottles, and meter sticks. Tell students they are going to work in pairs and submit a flight plan based on dead reckoning for a cross-country journey throughout the state in a Cessna 172. Describe a Cessna 172 as a four-seater airplane that can travel 126–167 miles per hour. Discuss the criteria involved for their flight as it is stated on Student Sheet 5.1. Ask how many different flight paths they think will meet the criteria. Develop the sense that no two flight plans will necessarily be alike.

Emphasize the need to conscientiously check data to ensure accuracy. You might ask what could happen if a pilot miscalculated the flight distance. Have students recall various methods introduced in previous activities for determining the direction and compass heading of a course-line. These might include

◆ Drawing a line heading north from the point of departure and using a circular protractor at this point to measure the direction

◆ Locating a meridian that crosses the course-line and using a circular protractor to measure its direction with respect to the meridian

Suggest that students apply any recommended technique to determine the compass headings. Tell them that using two different procedures on a given course-line can provide a check.

Circulate among the pairs of students as they are planning their routes, altering course-lines, and calculating data. As they complete their intended flight paths, suggest they look at other students' charts for comparison. Before students clean their maps for subsequent classes, be sure they have recorded sufficient information about their flight plans. Have them compare the flight plans to one on an aeronautical chart.

Aeronautical Charts. Distribute an aeronautical sectional chart to each pair of students. Have the students locate their city and other familiar landmarks. As they scan the chart, you may ask them to discuss some of the information a flight chart provides and to notice the scale, various symbols, and colors used. They may realize that the bold numbers, such as 108 and 63, indicate altitude. Yellow indicates cities, green indicates hillsides, brown denotes mountains, and magenta is used for roads. Notice that the intensity in color tends to correspond to an increase in altitude. Ask students:

◆ How does a chart compare to the laminated state map?

◆ Can you locate the compass rose symbols?

◆ How do they compare to other compass rose styles?

◆ Would your cross-country route look the same or different on an actual aeronautical chart? (Have students explain possible similarities and differences.)

◆ How might scale effect the appearance of the flight path?

Ask some pairs of students to use string or yarn and pins to plot their cross-country flight paths on aeronautical charts displayed in the classroom. Because portions of a state are either on different charts or opposite sides of the same chart, it may be necessary to align and connect at least two sectionals in order to represent the routes.

Discussion Questions

1. Altitude affects airspeed. The indicated airspeed is true only at sea level. The actual airspeed increases 2 percent for every 1,000 feet of altitude. A plane flying 200 miles per hour at 1,000 feet of altitude would actually be traveling 204 mph. At 2,000 feet, it would be traveling 208 miles per hour. What speed would this plane be traveling at 3,000, 4,000, 5,000, 6,000 and 12,000 feet of altitude? How can you calculate the actual airspeed for a plane flying 130 miles per hour at these altitudes? Test your hypothesis.

2. A Cessna 172 can maintain an altitude between 3,000 and 12,000 feet. For each leg of your state trip, determine a safe altitude to fly and adjust the airspeed and ETA based on this revised flight plan.

3. Find out the magnetic variations that apply to your state and adjust the true headings on your flight plan to reflect this correction.

Assessment Strategies

1. Exchange departure and destination points from your flight plan with another group. Chart and complete a flight plan for their journey. According to your results, does their flight plan satisfy the criteria? Explain.

2. A Cessna 172 holds 40 gallons of fuel and uses an average of 8 gallons per hour. A pilot considers a full tank of fuel to be equivalent to 4.5 hours of flying time. Why?

Radar

During World War I, pilots used a compass and their eyes to navigate. They would fly to one town, mountain, or other landmark, then use their compass to fly to the next landmark. This was called *pilotage*.

But what happened if fog hid the ground, or if the wind blew the pilot off-course, or if you wanted to travel over water (which doesn't have any landmarks)? These problems led to one of the most important developments of the war—radio detection and ranging, or *radar*.

A radar set sends out radio waves. When the waves hit an object, they bounce back to the radar. The time it takes for the waves to come back tell the radar how far away an object is. The direction in which the waves return reveals where the object is.

When the British first used their radar sets in planes, they found that the pilots could determine exactly what they were flying over by using the radar images. Towns reflect energy and appeared as bright marks on the radar scope. Water reflects the radar signal away from the plane, so oceans and lakes appeared as dark spots. Pilots could find coastlines, cities, and airfields much more easily with the help of radar. Best of all, radar worked at night and in any type of weather.

Today, radar can even detect nearby storms so pilots can steer around the bad weather. Radar is extremely important at airports. Air traffic controllers use it to trace the position of every plane in the air within 50 miles of the airport. They guide pilots on routes to avoid colliding with other planes.

Powerful radars are used to track satellites orbiting the earth and to study objects in the solar system. For example, by recording the echoes of radar waves sent to Venus, astronomers have been able to map Venus' valleys and mountains even though the planet is hidden from sight by thick clouds.

Investigate some of the other uses of radar. Write a one-page summary of your findings.

WASPs

Jacqueline Cochran took her first flying lesson in 1932. She was a successful beautician who would eventually own a prosperous cosmetics company. But it was that flying lesson that led Cochran to fame.

She quickly mastered the technology of aviation and became the first woman to enter the Bendix Transcontinental Air Race, which she won in 1938.

The British Air Commission heard of Cochran's fame as an outstanding pilot and asked her to train a group of women to be pilots for war transport service. When she returned to the United States, the Army asked her to start a similar women's pilot program. She was named director of the Women's Airforce Service Pilots, or WASPs.

The WASPs followed the same schedules as male flight cadets. They learned military training, physics, navigation, instrument flying, and advanced flight training.

At first, their duties were limited to ferrying, target towing, and tracking missions in the United States. But soon, the WASPs proved they could master the heavier aircraft, such as B-29s.

By the time World War II ended, 1,074 women had graduated from the WASP program. To meet these courageous women, Cochran toured all fifty bases where the WASPs were stationed. Cochran's WASP program ended as the war ended, but because of it, the opportunities for women pilots in the military began.

The State of Flying

Knowing how to navigate, you can fly from airport to airport throughout the country.

Before starting a cross-country flight, the pilot plans the flight thoroughly. This includes plotting the course on a chart, measuring distances, and computing compass headings, flight time, fuel usage, and estimated time of arrival. The plan must be approved by the Federal Aviation Agency station governing the airport at the starting location.

Plot a course and record the flight plan (see page 69) for a journey around the state in a Cessna 172 following these criteria:

1. Airspeed is 130 miles per hour.

2. Departure time is 9:00 A.M. and return time on the same day is 5:30 P.M.

3. You must land in at least four different locations, one each in the NE, NW, SE, and SW of the state.

4. You must remain on the ground for at least 15 minutes at each stop.

5. Land near the state capitol around 11:00 A.M. for a 45-minute lunch.

6. The third leg of your flight must be at least 1.75 hours.

7. A Cessna 172 holds 40 gallons of fuel and uses an average of 8 gallons per hour.

8. Round distance to tenths of miles.

9. Round time to hundredths of hours or convert to hours and whole minutes.

The State of Flying

Flight Plan

Depart Time	Location	Destination	Compass Heading	Distance	Fuel in Tank	Fuel Usage	Flight Time	Arrival Time
9:00 A.M.								

* Indicates a stop for refueling

FAMILY
ACTIVITY

PAPER PLANE
PREDICTIONS

Overview

Students and their families design paper airplanes. Based on the results of several test flights, each family determines its plane's average airspeed in feet per second. They represent their results graphically and then determine the time it would take their paper airplane to fly from home to school.

Purpose. Students and their families apply the concepts of distance, speed, and time to the aerodynamics of paper airplanes. Together, they realize the process an airplane designer uses to extrapolate information in order to make performance and flight predictions. Understanding the techniques involved in converting airspeed from feet per second to miles per hour reinforces and establishes equivalencies.

Time. Approximately three hours, following Activity 5.

Materials. *For each family:*

◆ Family Activity Sheets 1–4
◆ 8.5" × 11" paper
◆ Scissors (optional)
◆ Tape (optional)
◆ Carpenter's tape measure
◆ Stopwatch
◆ Calculator
◆ Straightedge
◆ Student Sheet 2.3 (optional, for reference)

For the teacher:

◆ Transparency Master
◆ Transparency pen

Getting Ready

1. Duplicate Family Activity Sheets 1–4.
2. Prepare Transparency Master and locate transparency pen.

Background Information

In this activity, students demonstrate to their families aspects of aeronautical navigation and what they have learned about the relationships among distance, speed, and time. Each family will construct a paper airplane and fly it to collect information concerning time and distance aloft. The families will make predictions, interpret their results, and form generalizations about the airspeeds of their paper airplanes.

The Great International Paper Airplane Contest is conducted annually. Paper airplane models are entered and judged in several different performance categories, such has distance flown, time aloft, and aerobatics. Recall that a plane's design reflects its purpose. A supersonic jet is built for speed, whereas a glider is constructed for soaring. See the Resources List (p. xiv) for more information on the contest and winning models.

The Writing Link "Navigating by Starlight" and the History Link "The Tuskegee Airmen" can be used at any time during this activity to stimulate student interest.

Presenting the Activity

Paper Planes. Ask students:

◆ Have any of you heard of the Great International Paper Airplane Contest?

◆ If so, what is it like?

◆ Have any of you entered it or known someone who has?

◆ Have any of you heard about other paper plane contests?

Discuss the different categories in paper plane contests. Discuss other types of planes and their functions. Emphasize that the design process to accomplish a specific goal requires several trials and modifications before completion, whether it's for a paper airplane or a Boeing jetliner.

Tell the class they are going to design a paper airplane with their families using a sheet of notebook paper. Their model should be designed for speed. Ask them how to determine the speed of an airplane. What information will they need? During the discussion, be sure students understand they need to make several test flights of their chosen plane, recording the distance flown and the time aloft, in order to calculate the plane's average airspeed.

The method used to launch a plane affects its performance and flight pattern. Suggest that families practice throwing the paper airplane several times before actually recording data. Remind them that a paper airplane can be easily damaged on a flight. Their families may be able to adequately repair the planes between trials, or they may need to actually remake the same model before continuing.

Distribute the Family Activity Sheets. Provide time for discussion and clarification of your expectations. Though the suggested time for this activity is three hours, the time required will vary from family to family. Give the students a reasonable time period, perhaps spanning a weekend, to complete the assignment. They will need this to arrange adequate family time to work on the project.

Explain that on the day the activity is due, they will display their planes in class. Each student will give a presentation to describe the experience and their results.

Use the Transparency Master to have students record their planes' data. As a class, analyze and interpret the compiled information.

Discussion Questions

1. Describe how you would run a paper airplane contest. What do you think is more important—speed, distance, or time in the air?

2. On the day of student presentations, before the family data is presented, discuss the following topics in groups:

   a. Did the method used to launch your plane affect its airspeed?

   b. How long does it take to walk to school?

   c. Do you walk slower or faster than your paper airplane flies?

3. On the day of their presentations, after the family data is presented, answer the following questions:

   a. Is the plane that flew the farthest also the fastest?

   b. Is the plane that flew the fastest also the one that stayed afloat the longest?

   c. Discuss the relations of speed, distance, and time in air. What could be some of the factors contributing to the observed results?

The Tuskegee Airmen

To the Germans they were known as the *Schwartze Vogelmenschen*, the Black Birdmen. To the rest of the world, they remained virtually unknown.

During World War II, African American organizations, along with many individuals, struggled to persuade the United States government to accept African Americans for training in military aviation. The government agreed to establish a test program in which African Americans would be trained in all aspects of military aviation and sent into combat as a segregated unit.

These aviators, who came to be known as the Tuskegee Airmen, were trained at an isolated complex near Tuskegee, Alabama. After their training, the Tuskegee Airmen joined the battle in Europe. Their brilliant combat records provided the evidence for the integration of the Air Force and eventually the full integration of the Armed Services.

In 1988 a statue of an African American World War II fighter pilot was dedicated at the Air Force Academy in Colorado Springs, Colorado, as a memorial to these brave men. Tuskegee Airmen, Inc., has created a scholarship fund that provides thousands of dollars each year to men and women of color seeking careers in aviation and aerospace. (For information about available scholarships, contact the Tuskegee Airmen Museum, Historic Fort Wayne, Detroit, Michigan.)

Navigating by Starlight

Tonight, when the stars are out, go outside and look up. Can you tell exactly where you are on the earth by looking at the night sky? Navigators over 3,000 years ago could, and fairly accurately.

At first, sailors watched how the stars moved in the sky throughout the year. They could judge north, south, east, and west by where certain stars appeared at certain times of the year. One star, the North Star, was particularly useful because it never strayed far from the northern pole. Sailors could even judge how far north or south they were on the planet by seeing how low or high the North Star sat above the horizon.

Sailors also used the sun as a navigating device. One instrument, called the kamal, was simply a short wooden tablet with a string through its middle. The observer would hold the tablet up to the horizon far enough from his face that the tip of the tablet touched the sun or star and the other end touched the horizon. Then he would pull the string up to his mouth and bite on it. The length of the string from the tablet to the observer's bite would tell the relative altitude of the sun or star. Then, using detailed tables, the sailors could determine what their latitude was on the earth.

Instruments such as the kamal eventually developed into sextants. Sextants measure the angular distance of an object in space above the horizon. After using the sextant, navigators use an almanac that tells the position of the sun, moon, stars, and planets at any given time during the year. With this information, navigators can calculate their course positions on a chart. Sextants are still used today on ships.

Explore celestial navigation (that's what you would be doing if you navigated using the stars or other objects in space). Research how a sextant works and how celestial navigation is used today. Write a one page summary of your findings.

Paper Planes

Materials Needed

- 8.5" × 11" paper
- Scissors (optional)
- Tape (optional)
- Carpenter's tape measure
- Stopwatch
- Scientific calculator
- Straightedge

1. Using 8.5" × 11" paper, design and construct a paper airplane that flies well.

2. Choose a place to fly and test your plane. Launch your plane at least five different times, each time measuring its time aloft and the distance it flies before landing. Record the results in the table below and calculate the airspeed for each trial.

Flight Tests

Trial	Distance in Feet	Time in Seconds	Airspeed in Feet per Second
1			
2			
3			
4			
5			

3. Explain how you could use the results in the table to calculate the average airspeed for your paper airplane.

4. The average airspeed of my paper airplane is _____ feet per second.

Paper Plane Predictions

1. Use your plane's average airspeed to express the distance your paper airplane would travel for the times listed in the table below.

Average Airspeed (Feet per Second)	Time in Seconds	Distance in Feet
	0	
	10	
	20	
	30	
	40	
	50	
	60	

2. Using Family Activity Sheet 3, graph the above relationship between time and distance. Label the horizontal axis for time and the vertical axis for distance in feet.

3. What do you notice about the points plotted on your graph? Connect them with a straightedge.

4. Explain how you could use your graph to estimate the distance your paper airplane would fly in 35 seconds.

5. Use your graph to estimate the time necessary for your paper airplane to fly 1,000 feet.

Time and Distance

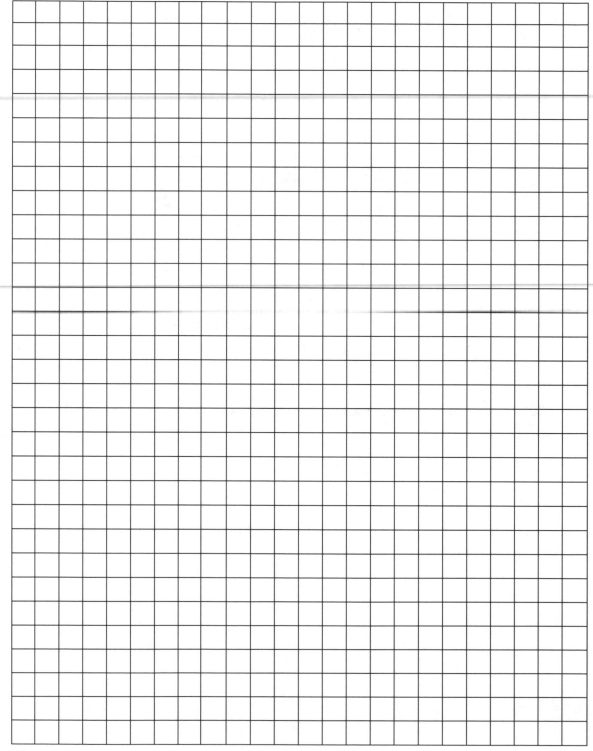

Flying to School?

1. You know the average speed of your airplane in feet per second. Calculate the average speed of your airplane in miles per hour.

   a. Your paper airplane's average airspeed is _____ feet per second.

   b. It flies _____ feet per minute and _____ feet per hour.

   c. There are _____ feet in one mile.

   d. If your paper airplane flies _____ feet per hour, then it flies _____ miles per hour.

2. How far is it "as the crow flies" from your house to school? This distance was estimated on Student Sheet 2.3, question 4b.

3. At this rate, how long will it take your paper airplane to fly from your house to school? Explain.

4. Would this be an efficient way to get to school? Explain.

5. What do you think is the maximum speed possible for a paper airplane? Explain.

6. Display on your paper airplane's wing its average airspeed in miles per hour. Bring you airplane, data, and graph to class.

Family Data

Name	Farthest Distance	Longest Time in Air	Average Airspeed
1.			
2.			
3.			
4.			
5.			
6.			
7.			
8.			
9.			
10.			
11.			
12.			
13.			
14.			
15.			
16.			
17.			
18.			
19.			
20.			
21.			
22.			
23.			
24.			
25.			
26.			
27.			
28.			
29.			
30.			

COMPLETED
STUDENT
SHEETS

City Maps

1. Locate your school on a city map. *Answers will vary.*

2. Is your school located in the north, south, east, or west part of the city? Explain.
   Answers will vary.

3. Using the city map, follow the written directions given to you. They begin at school and end at a familiar location.

   a. Describe the final destination.
   Answer should correspond to destination given in teachers directions.

   b. How did you know the destination?
   Answers will vary.

4. When you make a right turn, how many degrees are you turning? Explain.
   When you make a right turn, you are turning 90° by definition.

5. Choose a city park on the map. Its name is _Teacher's selection_.

   a. Is it north, south, east, or west of the school? Explain.
   Answers will vary.

   b. Write clear directions to travel by car from school to _Teacher's selection_ park.
   Answers will vary.

   c. Is there more than one route to this park? Why or why not?
   Answers will vary. One would expect multiple routes, but there could be exceptions.

   d. Determine the distance this park is from school. Explain.
   Answers will vary.

The Magnetic Compass

1. With your group, experiment with and examine the magnetic compass. Describe your findings.
   Answers will vary. Students should make reference to the magnetic needle, the symbols for the directions (N, E, S, W), the 360° circle, the index line, and the direction of travel arrow.

2. Follow these steps to orient yourself toward magnetic north.

   a. Turn the compass dial until the travel arrow is lined up with 0° (north).

   b. Stand up and hold the compass in your hand near the center of your body with the direction of the travel arrow pointing straight ahead. Keep the compass level so the magnetic needle can swing freely.

   c. While holding the compass, turn yourself around with the compass until the red north end of the magnetic needle points to the letter N on the dial.

   d. Look up in the direction of the travel arrow. You are facing north. Describe something in your room that identifies the direction north.
   The descriptors might vary, but they should all be in the northern part of the room.

   e. Do you agree with other groups? Why or why not?
   The descriptors might vary, but they should all be in the northern part of the room.

3. Follow these steps to orient yourself toward a heading of 60°.

   a. Turn the dial and line up 60° with the direction of the travel arrow.

   b. Stand and hold the compass as before with the direction of the travel arrow pointing straight ahead.

   c. Turn around until the red north end of the magnetic needle points to the letter N on the dial.

   d. Look up in the direction of the travel arrow. You are now facing a 60° compass heading. Give a descriptor (describe what you are facing) in your room that identifies the direction of 60°.
   The descriptors might vary, but they should all be in the same part of the room.

   e. A compass heading is read clockwise from north. Explain what this means.
   It's like reading a clock starting at twelve noon (north) and reading in the direction of one o'clock.

Compass Walk

1. With your group, use a compass to go on a walk around the path described below.

   a. Place a marker on the ground to represent your starting point.

   b. Orient yourself in the direction of a 50° compass heading. Walk ten paces and stop. Place another marker at this location.

   c. Orient yourself in the direction of a 160° compass heading. Walk ten paces and stop. Place another marker at this location.

   d. In what direction do you need to orient yourself in order to return to your starting point?
   285°. The results might be between 275° and 295° due to error in pacing and aligning the magnetic needle.

   e. How many paces do you need to walk in order to arrive at your starting point?
   Answers will vary between 10 and 12 depending on accuracy of pacing.

   f. Sketch a picture of your walk, including the angles of orientation (the compass heading) at each step.
   Answers will vary.

2. With your group, use a compass to walk the following path.

   a. Place a marker on the ground to represent your starting point.

   b. Orient yourself in the direction of a 40° compass heading. Walk ten paces and stop. Place a marker to designate your location.

   c. Orient yourself in the direction of a 220° compass heading. What direction are you facing?
   In the opposite direction.

   d. Walk ten paces and stop. Where are you? Explain.
   I am exactly where I started.

   e. Sketch a picture of your walk.
   Answers will vary.

3. What does this activity have to do with flying an airplane?
   Answers should have something to do with pilots knowing how to get where they want to go.

The Magnetic Compass

4. Adjust the magnetic compass and orient yourself to face

   a. due west. What is the compass heading? Give a descriptor of its direction.
   270°. Descriptors will vary depending on room arrangement.

   b. a 120° compass heading, and give a descriptor of its direction.
   Answers will depending on room arrangement.

   c. a 340° compass heading, and give a descriptor of its direction.
   Answers will depending on room arrangement.

   d. a compass heading of *Answers will vary*° (fill in the blank with a degree), and give a descriptor of its direction.
   Answers will vary.

   e. Check your descriptors with those of another group. Do they agree? Explain.
   Answers will vary.

5. Face a compass heading of 40°. Turn clockwise until you face the opposite direction.

   a. How do you know by looking at the compass that you have turned completely around?
   The direction arrow is pointing in the opposite direction. I initially aligned the magnetic needle with the direction arrow, both pointing N on the dial. When I turned around, the magnetic needle pointed S on the dial, which is the exact opposite of N.

   b. What direction do you think you are facing?
   Answers will vary. They probably will refer to SW.

   c. What is the compass heading? Describe how you can adjust the compass to give you the correct compass heading.
   220°. You need to move the dial until the magnetic needle matches up with the direction arrow. Then you read off the dial the degrees from north.

6. Refer to your city map. Approximately what compass heading will a plane face to fly from school to the city park you selected on Student Sheet 1.1? Explain your reasoning.
   Answers will vary with teacher's selection of park.

Compass Rose

1. A picture of a compass rose is given below. With your group, study and discuss it. Why do you think it is called a compass rose?

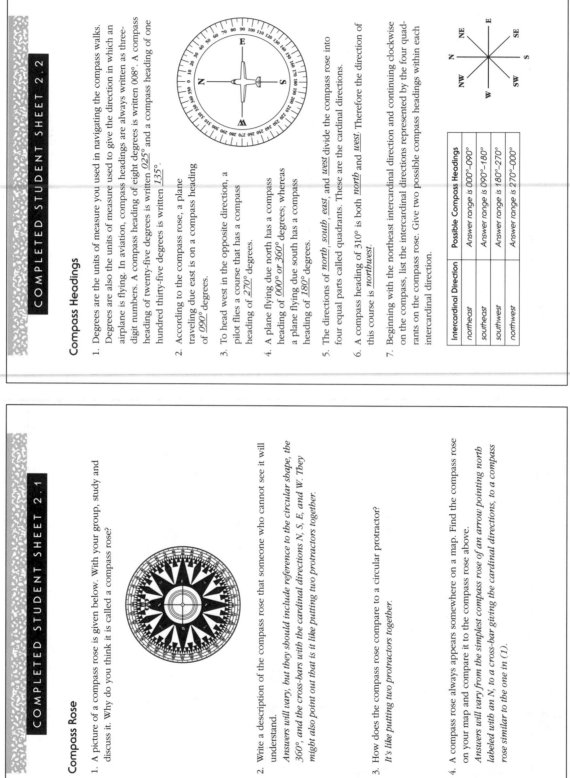

2. Write a description of the compass rose that someone who cannot see it will understand.
Answers will vary, but they should include reference to the circular shape, the 360°, and the cross-bars with the cardinal directions N, S, E, and W. They might also point out that is it like putting two protractors together.

3. How does the compass rose compare to a circular protractor?
It's like putting two protractors together.

4. A compass rose always appears somewhere on a map. Find the compass rose on your map and compare it to the compass rose above.
Answers will vary from the simplest compass rose of an arrow pointing north labeled with an N, to a cross-bar giving the cardinal directions, to a compass rose similar to the one in (1).

Compass Headings

1. Degrees are the units of measure you used in navigating the compass walks. Degrees are also the units of measure used to give the direction in which an airplane is flying. In aviation, compass headings are always written as three-digit numbers. A compass heading of eight degrees is written 008°. A compass heading of twenty-five degrees is written _025°_ and a compass heading of one hundred thirty-five degrees is written _135°_.

2. According to the compass rose, a plane traveling due east is on a compass heading of _090°_ degrees.

3. To head west in the opposite direction, a pilot flies a course that has a compass heading of _270°_ degrees.

4. A plane flying due north has a compass heading of _000° or 360°_ degrees; whereas a plane flying due south has a compass heading of _180°_ degrees.

5. The directions of _north_, _south_, _east_, and _west_ divide the compass rose into four equal parts called quadrants. These are the cardinal directions.

6. A compass heading of 310° is both _north_ and _west_. Therefore the direction of this course is _northwest_.

7. Beginning with the northeast intercardinal direction and continuing clockwise on the compass, list the intercardinal directions represented by the four quadrants on the compass rose. Give two possible compass headings within each intercardinal direction.

Intercardinal Direction	Possible Compass Headings
northeast	Answer range is 000°–090°
southeast	Answer range is 090°–180°
southwest	Answer range is 180°–270°
northwest	Answer range is 270°–000°

Flight School

1. On Student Sheet 1.1, you determined how to travel by car between your school and _same as on Student Sheet 1.1_ Park.

   a. Using a compass rose or a circular protractor, rewrite these directions using compass headings. Remember that a compass heading always reads clockwise from due North.
   Answers will vary, but they should contain the compass headings and distance.

   b. What do you notice about the compass headings? Explain.
   Compass headings designating a right turn (90°) and a left turn (270°) probably dominate.

2. Superman is going to fly from your school to this park.

   a. What is the compass heading for his flight to the park?
   Answers will vary.

   b. Estimate the distance of the flight.
   Answers will vary.

   c. What is the compass heading for his return flight to school?
   Answers will vary.

3. Locate another school on the map. It is _Answers will vary_. Write directions for Wonderwoman to fly from your school to the other school and back to your school.
   Answers will vary, but they should consist of just a compass heading and a distance.

Compass Headings

8. From the center of the compass rose, draw a course-line with a 010° compass heading. A 010° compass heading represents a northeast direction. Extend this same course-line in the opposite direction to describe a southwest heading of _190°_ degrees.

9. Use the indicated compass headings to draw course-lines on the compass rose. Extend each course-line to determine the compass heading in the opposite direction.

Compass Heading	Direction	Opposite Direction	Opposite Compass Heading
060°	northeast	southwest	240°
100°	southeast	northwest	280°
175°	south-southeast	north-northwest	355°
240°	southwest	northeast	060°
270°	west	east	090°
310°	northwest	southeast	130°
335°	north-northwest	south-southeast	155°

10. If you are given a compass heading, how could you determine the compass heading in the opposite direction without drawing the course-line?
Add or subtract 180°.

11. Use a circular protractor to determine the compass headings for the courses shown below.

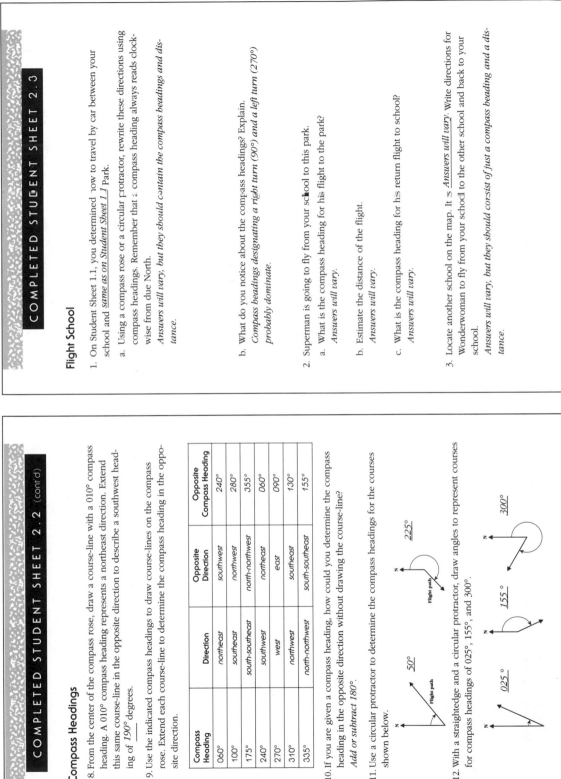

50°   225°

12. With a straightedge and a circular protractor, draw angles to represent courses for compass headings of 025°, 155°, and 300°.

025°   155°   300°

D, S, and T

All navigation involves three factors: distance (*D*), speed (*S*), and time (*T*). A pilot will know two of these and need to figure out the third.

1. A plane flying at 130 miles per hour (mph) will fly 130 miles in one hour.

   a. How far will this plane fly in half an hour? _65 miles_

   b. How far will this plane fly in two hours? _260 miles_

2. Complete the table to determine the distances flown from Olympia, Washington, to these other cities.

Destination	Speed	Time	Distance
Spokane, WA	135 mph	2.0 hours	270 miles
Richland/Pasco, WA	144 mph	1.25 hours	180 miles
Seattle/Tacoma, WA	130 mph	0.4 hours	52 miles
Portland, OR	132 mph	0.75 hours	99 miles

3. If you know the speed and time, how can you calculate the distance? *You can multiply speed by time to get the distance.*

4. A plane flying 150 miles per hour travels a distance of 75 miles. What is the flight time? Explain.

   Explanations will vary; one possibility is given.

   $$75 \text{ miles} \div 150 \, \frac{miles}{hour} = 75 \text{ miles} \times \frac{1 \, hour}{150 \, miles}$$

   $$= .5 \, hour$$

   The flight time is a half hour.

5. Complete this table to find the flight times from Salem, Oregon, to the various locations.

Destination	Speed	Time	Distance
Eugene, OR	130 mph	0.5 hours	65 miles
Bend, OR	132 mph	0.75 hours	99 miles
Pendleton, OR	136 mph	1.25 hours	170 miles
Yakima, WA	152 mph	1.25 hours	190 miles

Charting Courses

1. Locate three other airports on your state map. Chart a 40° course-line from each airport. Extend the course-lines for at least 100 miles. How are the three course-lines related?

   Answers should include the fact that the three course-lines are parallel.

2. How many 40° course-lines are there on this map?

   There are an infinite number of such course-lines, and answers should at the very least acknowledge that there are many of them.

3. If you and a friend fly at 120° course headings from two different airports within the state, where will you intersect each other?

   Since the two course headings are parallel, you will not intersect when flying within the state. Students may point out that near the north pole, the lines do intersect.

4. Discuss as a group the findings from questions 1 through 3 and their importance to aviation. Summarize the group's consensus below.

   Answers will vary; however, the essential fact is that same degree course-lines are parallel, and therefore, people flying on the same course-lines will not intersect (crash into each other).

D, S, and T

6. If you know the speed and distance, how can you calculate the time?
You divide the distance by the speed to get the time.

7. If you fly 1,000 miles in 4 hours, then you traveled *about 250* miles in 1 hour. What is your airspeed? Explain.
My airspeed is 250 miles per hour, which means my average speed for the trip is 250 miles each hour.

8. Complete the following table to determine the airspeeds for planes flying from Sacramento, California, to the following cities.

Destination	Speed	Time	Distance
Reno, NV	132 mph	0.75 hours	99 miles
San Francisco, CA	135 mph	0.6 hours	81 miles
Bakersfield, CA	134 mph	1.5 hours	201 miles
Los Angeles, CA	144 mph	2.5 hours	360 miles

9. If you know the time and distance, how can you calculate the speed? Explain.
You divide the distance by the time to get the speed.

10. **Distance, Speed, and Time.** If you know any two of these, explain how you can find the third.
Answers will vary, but a typical one is given.
If you remember the equation in any one of the three ways, you can then transform it to the equation you need to solve for the unknown.
For instance, I remember $S \times T = D$.
If I know T and D, in order to find S, I need the form $S = ?$.
Remembering $S \times T = D$, I divide both side of the equation by T to isolate S.
I have $\dfrac{S \times T}{T} = \dfrac{D}{T}$ or $S = \dfrac{D}{T}$.
Now I can find S by dividing D by T.

More D, S, and T

1. Work the three problems below and then discuss with your group how they are related.

   a. A plane flies 450 miles in three hours. What is its average speed?

   $$S = \frac{D}{T}$$
   $$= \frac{450 \text{ miles}}{3 \text{ hours}}$$
   $$= 150 \text{ mph}$$

   b. A plane flies 450 miles at a speed of 150 miles per hour. How long is the flight?

   $$T = \frac{D}{S}$$
   $$= \frac{450 \text{ miles}}{\frac{150 \text{ miles}}{1 \text{ hour}}}$$
   $$= 450 \text{ miles} \times \frac{1 \text{ hour}}{150 \text{ miles}}$$
   $$= 3 \text{ hours}$$

   c. A plane flies for three hours at a speed of 150 miles per hour. How far does it go?

   $$D = S \times T$$
   $$= \frac{150 \text{ miles}}{\text{hour}} \times 3 \text{ hours}$$
   $$= 450 \text{ miles}$$

2. Discuss with your group how the three questions are related and write a brief statement explaining the relationship.
   Answers will vary, but the response should refer to the fact that these three problems could all refer to the same trip, in each problem two different facts were given, and you had to find the third.

Paper Planes

Materials Needed

◆ 8.5" × 11" paper
◆ Scissors (optional)
◆ Tape (optional)
◆ Carpenter's tape measure
◆ Stopwatch
◆ Scientific calculator
◆ Straightedge

1. Using 8.5" × 11" paper, design and construct a paper airplane that flies well.

2. Choose a place to fly and test your plane. Launch your plane at least five different times, each time measuring its time aloft and the distance it flies before landing. Record the results in the table below and calculate the airspeed for each trial.

Flight Tests

Trial	Distance in Feet	Time in Seconds	Airspeed in Feet per Second
1	*Answers will vary.*		
2			
3			
4			
5			

3. Explain how you could use the results in the table to calculate the average airspeed for your paper airplane.
   Answers will vary, but should include process to calculate average.

4. The average airspeed of my paper airplane is _____ feet per second.
   Answers will vary, but should be consistent with process and given data.

Using D, S, and T

1. Calculate the expected airspeed if the course-line on an aeronautical chart measures 1,560 miles, and the flying time allotted is 12 hours.

$$S = \frac{D}{T} = \frac{1560 \text{ miles}}{12 \text{ hours}} = 130 \text{ mph}$$

2. A Cessna 172 has an average speed of approximately 155 miles per hour. You are asked to take it for a test flight 3.5 hours before sunset. What is the farthest possible total distance you can fly the Cessna and be sure to return before dark?

$$D = S \times T = \frac{155 \text{ miles}}{\text{hour}} \times 3.5 \text{ hours} = 542.5 \text{ miles}$$

This is assuming you want to be back at sunset. However, there is twilight between sunset and dark. So if one knew how to estimate that time, one could stay in the air longer, and go farther. It also assumes the plane reaches 155 mph immediately upon takeoff.

3. At 10:00 A.M. you are 2.5 hours into a 650 mile flight when advancing head winds cut your airspeed in half. If your airspeed at the start of the trip was 130 miles per hour, what is your revised estimated time of arrival (ETA)?

$$D = S \times T = \frac{130 \text{ miles}}{\text{hour}} \times 2.5 \text{ hours} = 325 \text{ miles}$$

$$650 \text{ miles} - 325 \text{ miles} = 325 \text{ miles}$$

$$T = \frac{D}{S} = \frac{325 \text{ miles}}{65 \text{ miles}} = 325 \text{ mph} \times \frac{1 \text{ hour}}{65 \text{ miles}} = 5 \text{ hours}$$

$$10:00 \text{ A.M.} + 5 \text{ hours} = \text{new ETA} = 3:00 \text{ P.M.}$$

4. As a group, pick two places in the state you would like to visit. Assume you will average 150 miles per hour in your Cessna 172. Develop and record a flight plan. What is the flying time to complete the visits and return home? Give the flying time first in tenths of hours, then convert it to hours and minutes.

Answers will vary, but they should include the course headings and distance from the location, the two selected places, and the return trip.